LOVE LETTERS

LOVE LETTERS

Let His Handwriting Be Your Guide

Cash Peters

CITADEL PRESS
Kensington Publishing Corp.
www.kensingtonbooks.com

CITADEL PRESS BOOKS are published by

Kensington Publishing Corp.
850 Third Avenue
New York, NY 10022

Copyright © 2003 Cash Peters

All Kensington titles, imprints, and distributed lines are available at special quantity discounts for bulk purchases for sales promotions, premiums, fund-raising, educational, or institutional use. Special book excerpts or customized printings can also be created to fit specific needs. For details, write or phone the office of the Kensington special sales manager: Kensington Publishing Corp., 850 Third Avenue, New York, NY 10022, attn: Special Sales Department, phone 1-800-221-2647.

CITADEL PRESS and the Citadel logo are Reg. U.S. Pat. & TM Off.

Designed by Leonard Telesca

First Printing: January 2003

10 9 8 7 6 5 4 3 2 1

Printed in the United States of America

Library of Congress Control Number: 2002113377

ISBN 0-8065-2477-4

How long do you have to date a man before you realize he's not the kind of guy you thought he was? Three months? Six?

In some cases it can take years to discover that, instead of a knight in shining armor, you've landed yourself a no-good, two-timing rat who's slowly wrecking your life. Of course, by that time it's too late—you've exchanged vows, and you're stuck with him till death do you part.

So how great would it be to know a few things about him *in advance*? To understand a little better how he thinks and feels *before* you invest time, energy and money in a relationship?

Well, finally you can! Within these pages, you'll find answers to questions women ask about their men. "Is he cheating on me?"— "Is he good in bed?"—"Does he have money?"—"Does he have a good sense of humor?"—"Is he gay?"—and hundreds more.

All you do is take a piece of his handwriting (more is better) and match up individual letters to the Love Letters in this book. In no time at all you'll build a sketch of what your guy is really like.

Try it. It's easy, very revealing, and, most of all, a whole lot of FUN!

So Many Secrets in Your Handwriting

Your handwriting gives away so much about you. Perhaps more than you'd like it to. Your personality, your behavior patterns, how you feel about yourself, your outlook on life, the way you handle stress or problems from your past, stuff that *really* makes you tick—it's all in there.

But how? That's the question I get asked more than any other: How come my handwriting reveals so much? The answer's simple.

Ever watched someone walk? Often, just by looking at the way he moves, you can tell what kind of person he is. Slow and casual, nervous and speedy, hot and bothered. Same when he eats: some folks gobble their food, others chew each mouthful forty times. Every one of us is a little package of energy—emotional energy, intellectual energy, sexual energy, and so on. More than likely, the guy who gobbles his food will do everything fast. He'll walk fast, talk fast, and yes, he'll *write* fast too.

Not only that, but the handwriting of someone who writes fast will have a lot in common with the handwriting of other people who write fast. Similarly, the writing of one guy with a spiky temperament will look a lot like the writing of another guy with a spiky temperament. A happy person has happy traits in his writing, sad people sad traits, and so on.

In short, handwriting analysis, done well, holds up a mirror to the soul.

A close friend of mine, Loveday Miller, is one of Britain's top graphologists (handwriting analysts). However, after studying the subject for over thirty years she was forced to conclude that, yes, the old-style techniques she'd learned were often right on the button, but they were also very complicated—*too* complicated in most instances for the everyday person to understand. There had to be an easier way!

And so, with Loveday's help, I set about devising a new method, one that almost anyone could use. As you can imagine, it took a while! But by researching thousands of pieces of writing, we finally put together a quite revolutionary system, one that links a person's behavior directly to the way he writes individual letters of the alphabet. It's so simple.

This system has been used successfully to analyze people and relationships in *Cosmopolitan* magazine, as well as on such TV shows as *Entertainment Tonight*, *The View*, *The Montel Williams Show*, and countless radio shows in Britain and America. Now you can use it too.

Love Letters may be the key to help you unlock secrets in your boyfriend's writing, or your husband's writing, or your best friend's, or even your own! Give it a try. You might be surprised by what you learn!

A few things you need to know before you get started

21 Useful Signs to Look Out For

The first time you pick up a piece of handwriting, before you begin examining individual letters, spend a minute or so taking in the overall look of it, because that can give you a lot of information right there.

SLOPES UP: Points to an upbeat nature. Expects things to turn out well. When slope is too steep, could mean extreme responses, perhaps hysteria.

SLOPES DOWN: Pressures weigh on his shoulders. He can't see the light at the end of the tunnel. He needs to resolve pressing problems.

SLANTS FORWARD: Sign of someone who gets on with life. Makes things happen. Doesn't waste time with excessive thinking, just does it.

SLANTS BACK: A reserved nature. The writer is thoughtful, cautious. Doesn't like committing to something before he knows the consequences.

 BIG WRITING: Larger than life on the outside; tender and vulnerable on the inside. His personality is his shield, his protection.

SMALL WRITING: Analytical, not prone to grand gestures. Often belongs to someone who enjoys working with figures or the minutiae of life.

SMALL AND CRAMPED: Writer's emotions are trapped. His spirit yearns to grow, explore, and express itself, but something holds him back.

SHARP AND SPIKY: Impatient with others. Demanding at times. Wants things now. Often, he won't listen to others. Believes his way is best.

LETTERS NOT CONNECTED: Sign of inner stress, control, a lack of trust in life. Not willing to ease up and go with the flow. Needs to relax.

MESSY: A lot of ideas and tasks compete for his attention. His focus switches from one to the next. There may be confusion and disorganization.

WIDE LEFT MARGIN: Cautious, slow to dive in. Considers options before taking plunge. Knows his place and doesn't like to overstep the mark.

WIDE RIGHT MARGIN: Afraid of letting people down. Tries hard to keep promises and beat deadlines. Completes tasks ahead of time.

LOOPS: Loops contain thoughts, worries, fears, reservations, options, ideas…the larger the loops, the more issues weigh on the writer's mind.

TAILS TO THE LEFT: Influences from the past still play a part today. Old pain, parental teachings, lessons learned in childhood—all have a bearing.

Roy Has	CLAWS AND HOOKS TO THE LEFT: Hanging on to the past. Emotional baggage. Won't or can't let go of old issues. Needs to break free.
I bET RadE	MIXED CAPITALS AND SMALL LETTERS: Not yet broken free of childhood. Still growing up finding his true voice. Unsure who he is.
So You	BIG CAPITALS, SMALL WRITING: A lot of his life is a performance. Inside, he's calmer, less outgoing, more contained. Not what he seems.
WHERE DO I GO?	PRINTING: A defense. In life, he tries to appear tougher, more competent, meaner, whatever, than he really feels. Could be weaker than you think.
bad petred	PLUNGING TAILS: A certain wisdom or knowing underlies his actions. He has more depth and understanding of life than he appears to have.

t AND h CLOSE TOGETHER: Sign of closeness in relationship. Mutually supportive, a good match. Too close and it could be smothering.

t AND h FAR APART: A lack of connection some or all of the time. Couple may be drifting apart, or maybe just don't understand each other.

7 Important Things to Bear in Mind

1. NOTHING CAN TAKE THE PLACE OF CHEMISTRY
   Handwriting offers a general guide only. If the writing says the guy's perfect, but your intuition tells you no, or your friends are screaming at you, saying he's a maniac, then **trust your intuition and your friends.** Be careful; it's a jungle out there. *Love Letters* **is no substitute for good judgment and common sense.**

2. DON'T BE AFRAID TO MIX AND MATCH
   A book this size can't include every possible variation on each letter of the alphabet, or it would be as heavy as a house-brick. So if, for instance, you come across an **A** in the writing and it looks a little like one example in the book but also a little like another,

then maybe the guy's a bit of each. Try combining them and read the two together.

3. OUR HANDWRITING IS ALWAYS CHANGING
It never stays the same. If you have a bad cold or you're stressed out right now, the way you write will deteriorate. That's just how it is. Conversely, if you're having a good day, there will be buoyancy to the writing, reflecting your mood. Take that into account when looking at a guy's handwriting. Don't judge too quickly or too harshly. Maybe he's just having a bad day.

4. HUMAN BEINGS ARE VERY COMPLEX
You must look at the overall picture. Interpreting one letter alone will not paint a full portrait. A single piece of handwriting may contain hundreds of letters, and even three or four variations on the *same* letter. A guy may write his **t** one way at the beginning of a word, another way in the middle, and an entirely different way when it's at the end. Each one will show up another subtle hue of his personality. Consider them as a whole.

5. BE KIND
You're sensitive. I'm sensitive. We're all sensitive about ourselves. Every guy you meet, even the rattiest of the rats, is, believe it or not, doing the best he can with what he has. Some fare less well than others, but they still deserve respect. *Love Letters* offers

you insights into how a person thinks and feels. That's a wonderful privilege. Don't abuse it. Be kind—always!

6. THERE ARE NO ABSOLUTES
   A system is only as good as the person using it. This is intended to be a general guide only. Think of it as a tool, not a bible.

7. HANDWRITING ANALYSIS IS A BLAST
   Have a great time with it. Enjoy the things you discover about your partner. Use them to make your lives better. Have fun!

How to Begin

STEP 1: GET HOLD OF THE GUY'S HANDWRITING.

- The best kind of writing is on unlined paper. That way, there's nothing to influence or restrict his flow. But if the paper has lines, don't worry; it should still work.
- The more handwriting you have, the more you can find out about him. Cursive is better than printing.
- Try to avoid anything pre-planned—memorized poems, old adages, or any of that quick brown fox jumping over lazy hens stuff. Letters, postcards, and spontaneously-written notes are preferable, something free-flowing. But if all you have is a poem, don't give up. Try using that.

STEP 2: THEN EITHER . . .

• Match letters in his writing one by one to those in the pages of the book. Read off their suggested meaning.

OR

• Find a question in the book that you'd like to know the answer to. For instance, "Is he scared of commitment?" The letter that reveals commitment issues is the **x**. Go to the handwriting, and look for an **x**. Match his **x** to one listed in the book and read off its suggested meaning. If he didn't write an **x**, don't despair. Check more letters. You may still be able to build up an adequate portrait.

Acknowledgments

How wonderful it would be if I could say I did all this alone. Really, it would. The truth is, I owe boundless appreciation to so many, for helping and encouraging me along the way.

First and foremost Loveday Miller—a dear friend, and one of the wisest, kindest, and most insightful handwriting analysts in the world today—for being a great sounding board always, as well as an incredibly patient mentor.

My agent. I'm not sure how much patience Job had, but Kristen Auclair must have three times as much. Her tenacity and enthusiasm, even when things go nuts, impress me constantly. I appreciate it more than you know, Kristen.

And then a bunch of great people who showed awesome faith during what I'll call my Wilderness Years. No need to go into details, but there's Gary Robertson (hurray!) and also David Austin, Raymond Bilbool, Len Richmond, Cheryl Glaser, Mandy Wheeler, Ellender Sahr, Adreana Robbins, Jeff Greenberg, and of course of course of *course* Stanley Penner.

Further details about **Love Letters,** other books by Cash Peters, any upcoming radio and TV appearances, and how to go about having your own handwriting analyzed, are available on:

www.cashpeters.com

LOVE LETTERS

a: Is he sensitive?

b: How is he with money?

c: Is he open-minded?

d: Does he have a temper?

e: Does he have a good sense of humor?

f: Is he outgoing?

g: Is he angry?

h: Is he spiritual?

i: Does he get depressed?

j: Can he take a compliment?

k: Does he enjoy intimacy?

l: Is he single-minded?

m: Is he cheating on me?

n: Can he keep a secret?

o: Is he kind and generous?

p: Is he optimistic?

q: Can he take criticism?

r: Is he dedicated?

s: Is he easygoing?

t: Is he in touch with his feelings?

u: Is he a party animal?

v: Is he good in bed?

w: Does he have good taste?

x: Is he scared of commitment?

y: Is he responsible?

z: Is he judgmental?

Sensitive? You have NO idea!

*See how big and round the **a** is. That tells you he's vulnerable. Oh sure, he may try to hide it, pretending that he's not hurt and it's water off a duck's back. Some guys even overcompensate by throwing their weight around a little too much. But it's probably all for show and underneath he's a kitten. Be extra kind and nurturing. Let him know he can drop the façade with you.*

Is he sensitive?

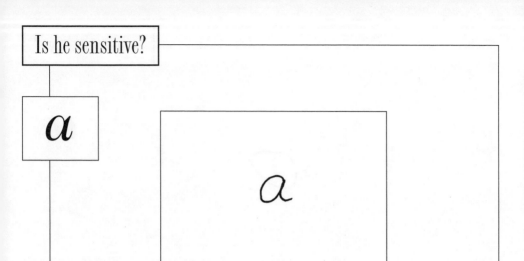

Sensitive up to a point

A relatively straightforward person who weathers life's little storms okay. It's not that he doesn't have a sensitive side—so try not to go too far with your criticism—but there's a reasonable level of resilience here, so he's unlikely to overreact if you tell him a few home truths. He may be crushed inwardly, but he'll try not to show it.

a

a

Shielding his emotions

Some people were so hurt, or felt so betrayed and let down when they exposed their sensitive side that they've taught themselves not to do that anymore. This guy has built a shield over his feelings to protect them. "Enough and no more," he's saying. "I will not go through that again." It's a matter of trust. It could take some effort to crack the shell, but hey, there may be gold buried under there!

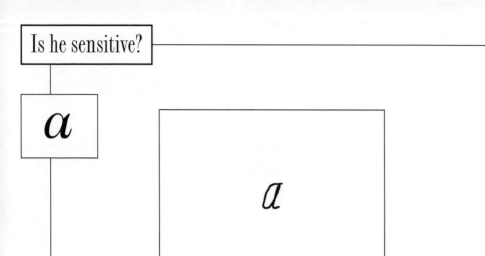

The Punchingbag

*He's had his nose put out of joint more times than he can remember. Now he's so used to it that he almost expects it. The flattened look to the **a** shows that his resilience has been weathered down, so be careful what you say. It's too easy to hurt him. The wrong word at the wrong time could cut his confidence to the bone.*

a	Tough nut to crack; afraid of opening up
a	Matter of fact; will consider comments and suggestions
a	Flying under the radar; hard to be certain what he's up to
a	Withdrawn; hides feelings, acts in his own good time

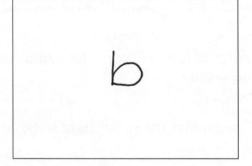

Money in the bank—and out again

*A big, fat old **b** like this one often belongs to someone who loves making money and loves spending it too, a guy who may be prudent with his cash, but is not afraid of putting it to good use. Of course, you may have bagged the one rich man with a large **b** who won't part with a penny. If so, that's hard. But this is not a miserly **b**. You could be in luck.*

b

Average

Generally okay with his cash. Even if he's not a bigshot and doesn't have stacks of dough, and even if he insists on treating what he does have with respect, it could be fun trying to get him to buy you something. Ask yourself: do I really need that Mercedes convertible, or could I make do with a Honda?

b

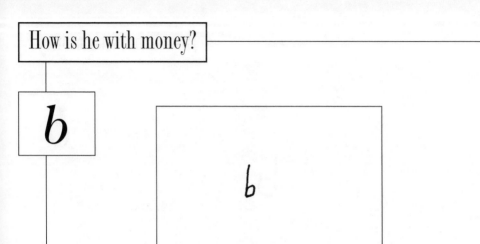

Mr. Scrooge

Way too sensible, way too cautious. He's unlikely to part with a penny unless he has to, and if he's like that with money, what else is he going to be tight with? If "lavish" is your middle name, your lifestyle, your spending habit, and your goal for the future, this guy may not be for you.

b

The Leaky Bucket

Money's coming in, but where's it going? It seems to dribble away with nothing to show for it. This guy either thinks big and earns small, or he has too many commitments and lives beyond his means. It may not be his fault. But that's no good to you, is it? He believes he deserves more, but does he have the guts to ask for it?

h   Can't make ends meet; needs to get organized

b   Knows what to do with money; could he have secret stash?

b   Always looking; stay alert to his intentions

b   Careful; thinks first, spends later

c

C

Free and easy

Well, okay, maybe not that easy. But when the "mouth" of the **c** *is wide-open like this, chances are his mind will be too. He'll try new things, be open to fresh ideas, and willing to change his opinion if he hears a more convincing argument. This guy wants to learn and could be knowledgeable and fun.*

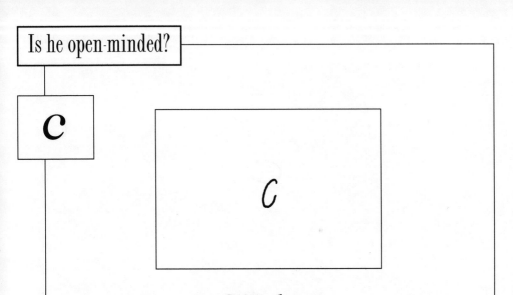

Is he open-minded?

c

Critical eye

*A narrow **c** indicates a sharp mind with strict standards. He sorts the wheat from the chaff in any situation and knows exactly what he likes, discarding anything he doesn't. It's hard to pull the wool over his eyes. He observes, he decides quickly, and moves on. In short, if you make it past the second date, give yourself a pat on the back. It means you passed the test!*

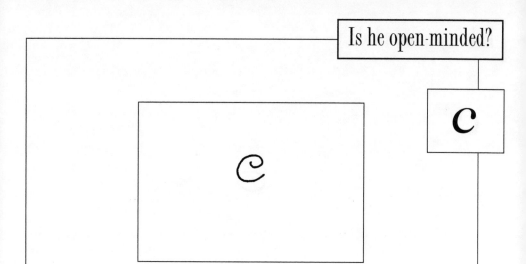

Blocked

*A curl-around on the top of the **c** means he'll have strong opinions on certain issues. The more pronounced that curl, the stronger and more immovable those opinions are likely to be, and possibly the more cynical he'll be too. Don't argue with him. Once he makes up his mind that he's right, that's the end of it. Even when he's wrong.*

C

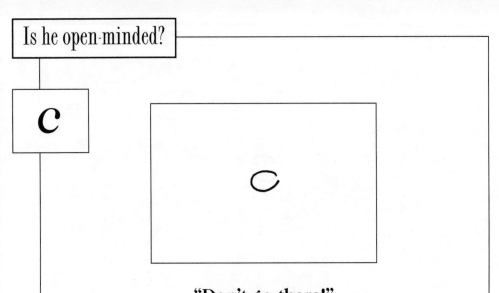

"Don't go there!"

He is very selective about the kind of information that he accepts. He's learned to be circumspect and to analyze instructions, data, statistics, whatever comes his way, rather than taking it all on trust. This may stand him in good stead in terms of not being duped, but by focusing on details, is he missing something more important?

𝒞   Closed off; ingrained attitudes, possible prejudice

𝒞   Eager to learn; constantly after knowledge; you need to BE FASCINATING!

𝒞   Can't see the forest for the trees; swamped, burdened; limited view

𝒞   Sneaky; could be cunning, persistent; thinks he can have whatever he wants

d

Short fuse

*Growl, snarl, snap, grrrrrrr . . . this probably isn't the type of guy you can mess with. He can be very impatient at times. Incompetence irritates him. Delays irritate him. Broken promises irritate him. Or just wearing your hair all wrong. Let's face it, on a bad day almost **everything** rubs him up the wrong way. Okay, so his bark's worse than his bite—but who wants to be bitten at all?*

d

Clark Kent

*An average-sized bowl on the **d** together with a straight, un-looped stem points to an even temperament. He may have his breaking point, and could become testy, but treat him well and he should be a darling the rest of the time. There's a pleasant person in there, someone who doesn't have an axe to grind. Should you get him while he's fresh?*

d

The Saint

No doubt he seems even-tempered, understanding, and long-suffering. Insult him, abuse him, nag him—you think he can take it all. Then one day, when it all gets too much—BOOM!—he blows. When he does, run for your life. He's good for the long haul possibly, and under it all may be a heart of gold.

d

Concealed issues

The looped tail points to an accumulation of deep thoughts, fears, and even resentments. The bigger the loop the greater the build-up of petty irritants and the more likely he is to express them. Someone with a large looped tail usually finds a lot of things to trouble him. It may not take much to set him off. Make sure you're not in the line of fire when he does.

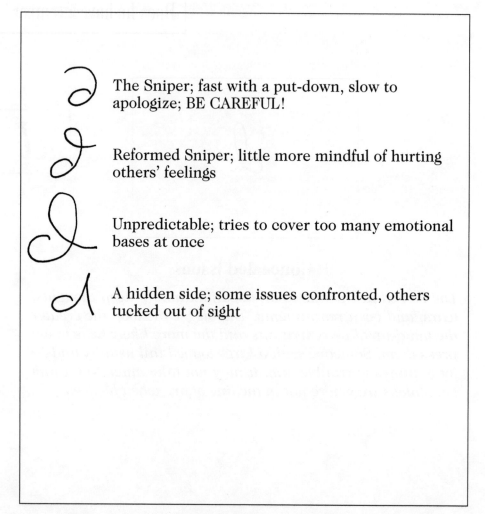

The Sniper; fast with a put-down, slow to apologize; BE CAREFUL!

Reformed Sniper; little more mindful of hurting others' feelings

Unpredictable; tries to cover too many emotional bases at once

A hidden side; some issues confronted, others tucked out of sight

e

Happy, happy, happy

Look at that sonuvagun go! Note the way it appears to be grinning. Here's someone who enjoys life. He'll probably have a winning smile and love to laugh, often at stupid things that just catch his funny bone. That's part of his charm and he knows how to use it. If a sense of humor matters to you, this one could be quite a catch.

Eager to please

He likes to be liked. Maybe he cracks jokes all the time, or maybe he just giggles helplessly at comments you make—even the unfunny ones. There's deep need within him to belong and to be appreciated. It's possible he tries way too hard to fit in at times, which is great if you're looking for a doormat. Otherwise, his antics could grow old fast.

e

Look at this dumb thing I just did!

*The fact that the **e** comes around and sweeps backward indicates that the guy sees the funny side of life, even his own inadequacies. Some of the most traumatic events in life have a humorous side, something you can laugh about later. "I just broke my Dad's priceless Ming vase! Hahahahaha!" Giggle with him to your heart's content.*

Look at that dumb thing you just did!

*He gets a kick out of others' misfortune—from the other guy falling down an open manhole or walking into a door. A bit juvenile, but hey, at least **he's** enjoying himself. Is he mean-spirited? Probably not. On the other hand, he does like to see those who have wronged him get their comeuppance. Make sure you're not one of them.*

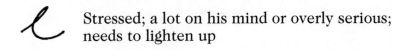 Stressed; a lot on his mind or overly serious;
needs to lighten up

Intense; limited emotional range; needs to
nurture the heart

Ouch!—prickly exterior, mischievous or even
malicious as form of defense

Sharp retorts; don't back him into a corner; see
what happens once he cools down

f

Dances on tables

*A large bottom loop points to bags of personality. But he could be fun **all** the time, which may be tiresome, especially if you're not in the mood. The guy just can't help it. He doesn't care what people think of him. If he gets the urge to run butt-naked down Main Street, he'll probably do it. The bigger the loop, the truer this is likely to be. The smaller the loop, the less outgoing.*

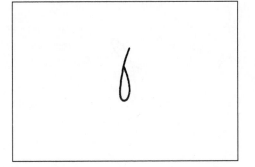

Knows when enough is enough

This guy has fun on his own terms. It's not necessary for him to be laughing and singing the whole time. If that's what he feels like, great. Otherwise, he does what he wants when he wants. Once he's had enough fun, the serious side of his character kicks in and he'll want to go home. This may seem selfish to some, but he's just doing things at his own pace.

f

Why is everybody looking at me?

This guy cares a lot what people say about him. The fears wrapped up in that big top loop tend to inhibit him in certain circumstances, preventing him from doing things he would otherwise do. If only he could relax more and care less. Perhaps it's time to smell the roses and realize what's important in life.

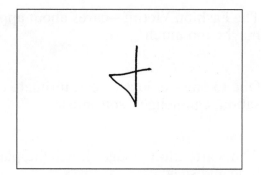

The Belle of the Ball

Loves to be the center of attention, adores partying, and longs to be seen with the right people. Most likely, he'll arrive fashionably late and leave depressingly early—anything to show he's important—and won't care what others think about him. Given the chance, he'll outsparkle the whole room. Some people just have the knack, and this guy's one of them.

The Fashion Victim—cares about appearances, maybe too much

 One to one—enjoys direct, intimate conversation, candlelight, soft music

 Wants attention, dodges limelight; plays social hide and seek

 Just plain shy; blown off one too many times? Want to try to give him hope?

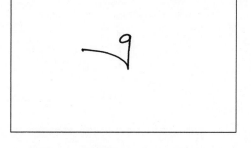

Sharp and to the point

*The tight little head on this **g** and that sharp, accusing tail tell you to handle this one with kid gloves. He has a point to make and he's not afraid to tell it like it is. Or rather, as he sees it. He can be impatient and possibly aggressive. When he witnesses a wrong, he'll want to right it, often doing so before he's thought through the consequences. Don't take it personally.*

33

g

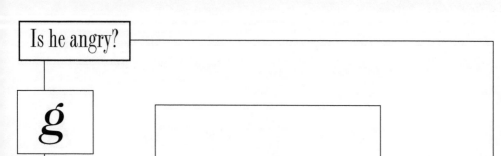

Irritated, but you're not sure why

A tight little head suggests a measure of impatience and even withheld aggression. If he's annoyed, you may not know why. It's possible he lacks the courage to walk up to people and have it out with them. Whether he does or he doesn't, expect him to fume inwardly and make snappy comments. Then it's over. Until the next time.

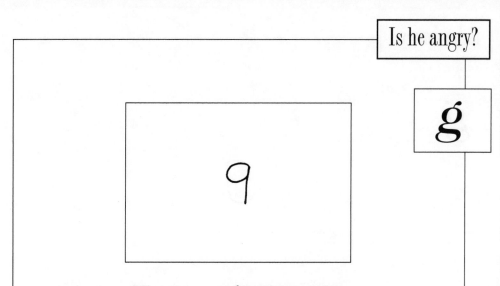

g

Nice . . . perhaps too nice

A sensitive type who does not enjoy direct confrontation. He'd far rather absorb his bad feelings and not react too quickly in case he starts what he can't finish and becomes embroiled in a bitter battle. If he's driven to frustration or fighting back, he may vent this in angry letters or emails, or even poetry and novels, but seldom to the face of the person who offended him.

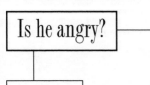

Is he angry?

Balanced responses

Probably a nice, reasonable guy who takes adversity in stride and doesn't get too upset by off-color comments or other people's bad behavior. But he'll only take so much. He wants to be nice, and tries hard to get along with everyone, but he's aware the meek won't inherit the earth. Push him too far, and he's not beyond telling it like it is. Good for him!

g Withheld grievances; you may think he's over something, but maybe not; the larger the bottom loop, the more grievances

g Emotional game player; out to win any battle and give opponents comeuppance

g Has aversion to blame or criticism; be sparing with negative comments

g Sulky; when upset, tends to go over and over same ground

Is he spiritual?

h

Has a spiritual side

That loop on the stem of the h *is filled with thoughts and questions about life. The bigger it gets, the deeper his yearning to know and understand. "Is there a God?"—"What are His plans for me?"—"Is there life after death?"—or a hundred others. He's pondering the meaning of existence here, looking for answers.*

h

h

The Idealist

The taller the stem, the more the person reaches for higher principles. He sees beyond the present and seeks something better, either for himself or for the world. We have a name for people like this: we call them dreamers. They stand on an elevated plane and look out over our heads. But are they wise or foolish?

h

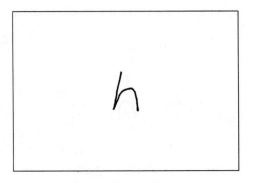

Simply happy

Enjoys life for what it is and as it is, and doesn't dig much deeper than that. It's not that he's not interested, he may well be, but there's a lot of childlike innocence here. Delve too deep, he thinks, and some of the rosy glow might disappear. He may take too many things for granted and exist on superficial levels. But if he's happy that way, why try to change him? He'll learn soon enough.

Maturing and beginning to look deeper; probably not a lot of interest in wider issues

 Guards what he believes very carefully; doesn't require your input, thank you

 May tell you he has everything figured out, but has a long way to go (Quit trying to change him before you even begin.)

 Searching and experimenting, but there's distance between where he is and where he ought to be

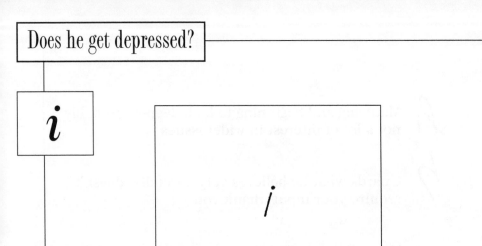

Up one minute, down the next

A dot hugging the top of the i means he tends to view life's events from close up. Little setbacks get magnified. Minor criticism cuts him to the quick. He tries hard to get things right, so failure or rejection, which are just signs that something he's doing isn't working and needs to be revised, make him question his own worth. His moods will probably vary according to the kind of day he's having.

i

Fairly average

*The **i** is dotted the usual way, not too close and not too far from the stem. That's fine. If he gets knocked down, he'll most likely get back up, dust himself off, and carry on. We all have our "down" moments; what matters is how fast we recover, learn the lesson that's embedded in defeat, and move on. This guy takes setbacks seriously, but rarely so seriously that they become debilitating.*

i

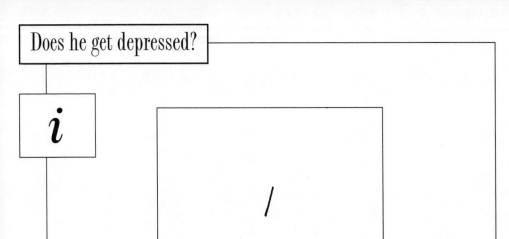

Who's got time to be depressed?

There's no dot here at all—sign of a very busy mind. There's so much going on that he daren't focus for too long on mistakes or setbacks. Maybe it's deliberate. Keep busy, and avoid experiencing doubts or moods. He may seem scatter-brained or to have too many balls in the air. When your mind's this active, there's no room for gloom.

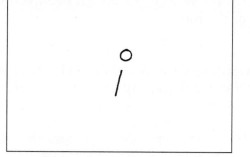

i

You cradle-snatcher!

Yes you! The circle above the i denotes boyhood innocence, and, in a man, possibly a strong feminine side. If he's young, it means he's naïve and as yet unjaded by the travails of life. However, if he's over forty and still drawing circles (or hearts!) over his i's, you may find you're dating the Tom Hanks character from Big.

/ • Always looking ahead; an occupied mind shrugs off the blues

/ ⟨ Gathering information, constantly evaluating, whether driven by fear or dedication

• / The past isn't over yet; issues that should be dead and buried can still preoccupy

/ ⊂ Concerned about tomorrow; what might happen can bring him down more than what *is* happening (Keep him away from horoscopes!)

46

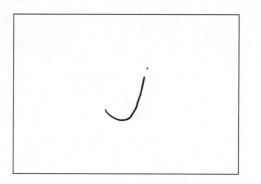

Fishing for compliments

Look at the hook! The way it reaches around to catch every last droplet of praise. "How did I do? Was I okay? Do you approve? Did I pass?" He needs reassurance and kind words the way margaritas need tequila. If he tries hard and earns it, great. But it's possible he's just plain insecure. Perhaps he had overcritical parents, or never received any praise as a child. Now he needs a lot.

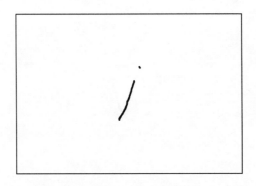

Wishing and hoping . . .

*. . . for any crumb from your table. A kind word, a thought-ful thank-you, a small token of your appreciation. Anything will do. Like a satellite dish, this **j** is waiting to receive con-gratulation signals. The man is needy, and may not even re-alize it. The question is, can he distinguish between fake praise and the real thing?*

j

No B.S.

He's no fool. More than likely, he knows his own worth. Compliments when they're deserved will be accepted and appreciated. But make it sincere and don't lay it on with a trowel. Some people depend on praise to keep their self-esteem afloat, while others are self-contained—all they need is "am I doing okay and am I heading in the right direction?" This guy is the latter.

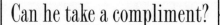

Can he take a compliment?

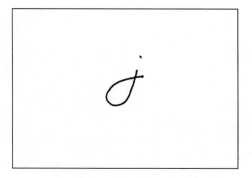

Keep it short

Expect this man to be full of himself. Or, if not that, either ultra-cynical or the type who doesn't fully trust anyone who praises him. "Yes, yes, yes, okay, I'm wonderful—now can we move this along please?" If he gets a pat on the back, it had better be an Academy Award at least. Anything less and he's not interested.

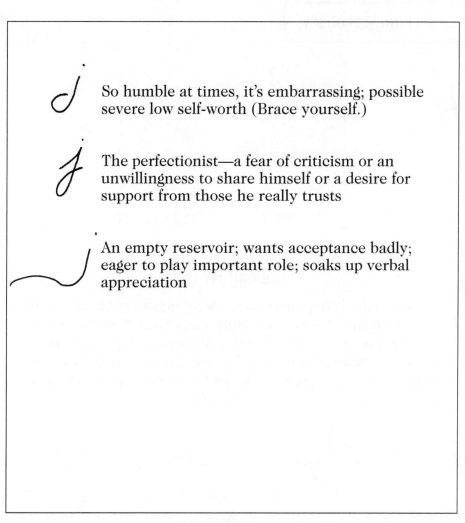

ʤ So humble at times, it's embarrassing; possible severe low self-worth (Brace yourself.)

ʄ The perfectionist—a fear of criticism or an unwillingness to share himself or a desire for support from those he really trusts

ʝ An empty reservoir; wants acceptance badly; eager to play important role; soaks up verbal appreciation

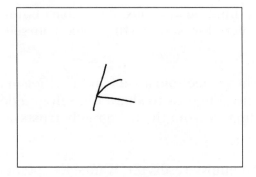

Hugs all round!

You can tell, just by the way those arms reach out to the right, that he seeks affectionate responses. Unless the outward signs say different, then he enjoys hugs and is not afraid of physical contact. In fact, he may need intimacy quite badly and go full-out to find a warm body to share his love with. Likely to be sincere and loving.

52

k

k

Unsure

It's about trust and not wanting others to get too close to him too quickly. Either he has a fear of giving up his emotional independence, or he may be the type that suspects everyone of being out to get him, so he protects himself, not letting anyone in. By keeping people at bay, he can control situations and won't get swept away. But by being too rational about love, he's missing out.

k

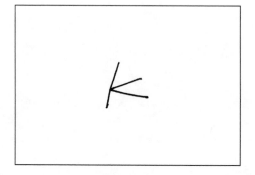

Needs hugs

He's not inhibited, far from it; yet there are certain control issues that need to be overcome before he will feel totally comfortable. He enjoys shows of affection, but he probably feels there's a time and a place for everything, and it has to be with the right people. Once he relaxes and gets to know you, he'll be more at ease.

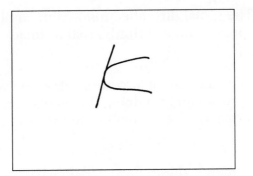

Demonstrative

*The largeness of the **k** tells you he needs big-time reassurance and big hugs. Cuddling, closeness, kisses—he'll probably take anything he can get. Indeed, try to stop him. If he's like other big-**k** people, he'll be all over you before you've said "hello." It's probably hard not to like him, but he could overwhelm you.*

The social flirt; affectionate but can be insincere; spreads himself thinly; real intimacy scares him

 Slick and quick at getting what he wants; can seduce you into doing things his way—make sure all's above board before saying yes

 Demands things now; will do whatever it takes to let you know who's boss; could be a power struggle

 Super needy; tries to fill emotional void by seeking affection, reassurance, love, encouragement (Get ready to give, give, give.)

l

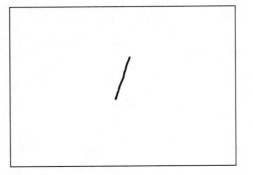

Knows what he wants

He is goal-oriented. Not the type to be thrown off course easily. Wherever possible, he makes a commitment, sets his sights, and pursues whatever he wants till he gets it. So if your love happens to be his goal, expect roses at your door, minstrels under your window . . . whatever it takes to make you say yes. The next move is yours.

l

Nothing is impossible

*Contained within that loop are big plans and all kinds of fascinating possibilities. Because it's tall, it feels like he's reaching for the sky. And the sky really is the limit, as far as this guy's concerned. If he can focus his energies, set a firm course, and back his dreams with committed action, he can move mountains. The smaller the **l**, the less ambitious he'll be.*

l

Underachiever

Could do more, but doesn't. Could aim higher, but won't. Should be all kinds of things he isn't. Something's getting in the way. He's lost the motivation, or maybe he never had it. Whatever the problem is, it looks like he's stuck in a rut. Someone needs to light a firecracker under his dreams and get some action going before the good years are gone and it's too late.

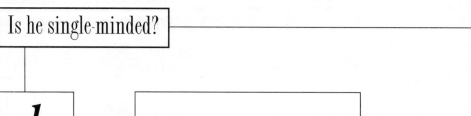

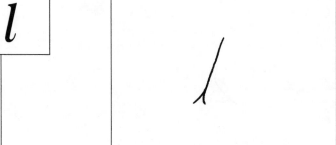

Shaky foundations

*The **l** is too tall. Either his ambitions exceed his talents, or his commitments exceed the time available to complete them. He's someone who spreads himself too thinly. It's time to return to basics. Cut away the dead wood, slow down, reconsider options. He should build a firmer base under his dreams, or they could all come tumbling down.*

His past hinders progress; early influences still play in his head; has to find his own voice

 Disillusioned, needs sympathy and understanding from someone who believes in him

 So much time, so little focus; by being too many things to too many people, he wastes energy

 Frustrated; maybe big plans got him nowhere; maybe he's done all he can in present position; focus and action are needed

m

The Rat

*A three-loop **m** means shared love. Looks like two separate people have a strong hold on his heart, and he doesn't know which one to pick. Before you go charging in, making accusations, be sure that third person isn't his mother. Having an extra loop on the **m** doesn't always signify infidelity. But sometimes it does—which is enough to keep you wondering.*

m

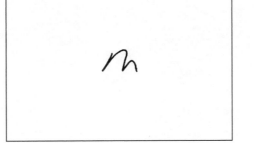

Open to offers

*A small right hoop on the **m** means he probably has no one of major importance in his life right now. Or if there is a current partner, the flame of love may be dying. If you've been dating this guy and you're the current partner, it could indicate that you don't mean as much to him as you thought you did. Time for a serious Q&A.*

m

Young and foolish

*A sharp, pointy **m** betrays certain juvenile traits. He refuses to grow up. He likes his partner to be his friend, because he understands friendship, but he's not mature enough or relaxed enough yet to enjoy a fully mutual adult relationship. That may affect his commitment too. If you enjoy his brand of little boy charm, wonderful. Need something deeper and stronger? Start looking around.*

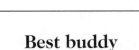

Best buddy

*An **m** with small hoops, or none at all, tells you that the guy is looking for a friend and companion, someone to laugh and have a good time with, someone who shares his interests. Depth of feeling is not his specialty. Commitment to one person might not be on the menu either. He's looking for a woman to be like another one of his guy friends. Fun, but hard to go deep with.*

Lessons and principles from childhood won't go away; you're living with him *and* his family

 Looking for a partner to take the reins; either he'll idolize you or let you do most of the work

 Lovey-dovey; certainly has the potential for unerring devotion

 Too much closeness? could cling too tightly, sorting out issues could take a long while
(Need to come up for air?)

n

n

Quite private

*An **n** that looks like a tunnel entrance tells you he keeps information to himself. He may not have anything sinister to hide, he's just not the type to broadcast everything about himself. If he wants you to know, he'll tell you in good time. Which means that he can probably keep a confidence, or be trusted not to go blurting out your private details to all and sundry.*

67

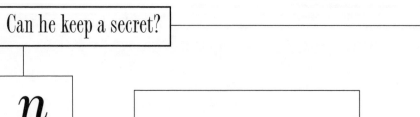

n

Guarded

He protects his territory. Privacy is important to him, and so is his intellectual property. He takes care of what he knows and retains certain information about himself that he'd prefer not to share with the rest of the world. You may think you have a right to know; apparently he disagrees. A cagey kind of guy. That may make him all the more intriguing.

n

Kiss and tell

*An open book. All you have to say is, "Now, this is in the strictest confidence, okay?" and the very next day it'll be all over the neighborhood. Can't keep a secret for long, if at all. Even as you open up your heart to him, he'll be mentally listing the people he's going to tell. So if it's really a secret, **don't** tell him.*

69

n

μ

Deliciously indiscreet

There don't seem to be any rules here. Everything is fair game—his own life, other people's, yours. Once he starts talking he just keeps on and on, being wonderfully forthright and honest, and not caring who hears his news. On one level such openness is great; on another, if you told him anything in confidence, your secrets are at risk.

Separate private and public faces, subjects he will or won't talk about (If your secret's important, keep it to yourself.)

 Reserved; not always happy to speak his mind; could be charmingly bashful or annoyingly coy

 Doesn't want to be put on the spot; won't answer direct questions; if you push, will look for someone less inquisitive

 Firm boundaries, don't push him too far; could come around in his own good time—be patient

Is he kind and generous?

O

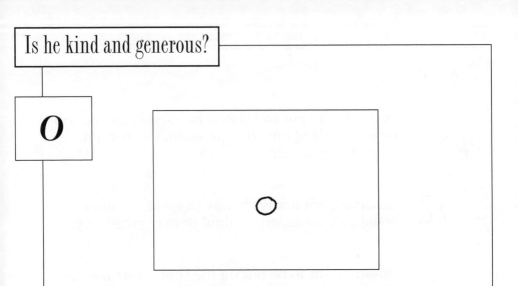

Sweetie pie

A full round o is a sign of a sensitive, giving nature. It can also point to a man with a strong feminine side. Does that mean he's gay? It might. But straight men can also have a softer, more caring aspect to their nature. Maybe he's just open, approachable, trusting, and unusually emotional. Whatever he is, he will not respond well to harsh words.

O

o

Tight

*A tight **o** often signifies a tight wallet. Here's someone who watches the purse strings, keeps the checkbook balanced, and probably monitors income and expenditure like a hawk. Problem is, it can also mean suppressed feelings. Someone who understands the bottom line but not the ways of the heart. May be unadventurous in love.*

O

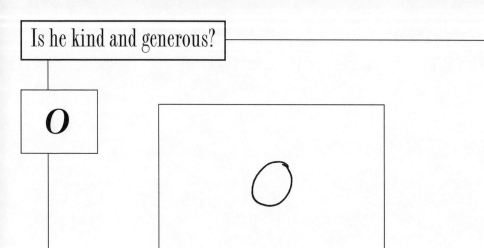

Gives too much, feels everything

He gives because he needs to receive. The bigger the o, the truer this is. It shows overextended emotions, a heart that is worn right there on the sleeve, a tenderness and vulnerability that can be hurt in an instant. He can never get enough love or understanding to satisfy his needs. He feels pain easily, and may protect himself by putting on a big, loud front.

O

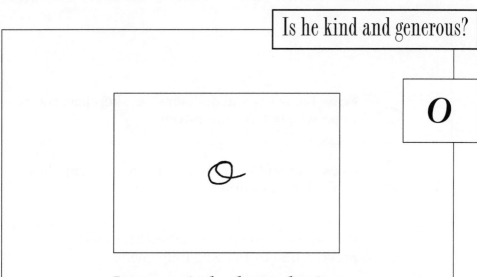

In two minds about sharing

*A part of him likes to be involved and to open up, but at some deeper level he really wants to be left alone. The **o** is divided into two parts. Beneath the external person lies someone else, a shyer individual who's unsure how much to give of himself. Should he let people in completely, or hold back? Doesn't fully trust anyone.*

Fears being exploited; defensive, skeptical, wants to be sure before committing.

Goes over and above what's necessary; supplies vital support to others.

Running for cover; restrictions (his own?) prevent him from being fully giving

Tension and fear; looking for reassurances while feeling pinned down or hemmed in

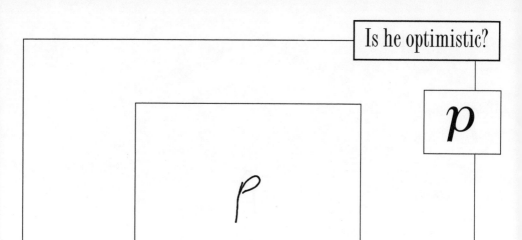

Expects good things

*A perky **p** is a good sign. He tries to see the best in any situation. That doesn't mean he won't have bad days, but he'll probably handle them better than most. There's an undercurrent of upbeat expectations with this person. He evaluates situations and problems with a can-do attitude. Useful to have around.*

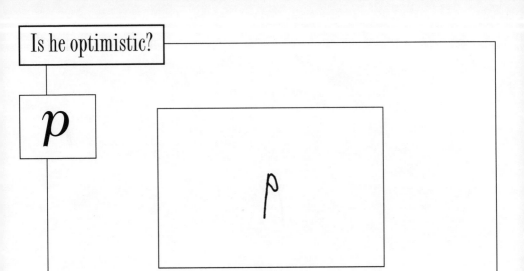

Obstacles are getting to him

This little guy feels defeated, maybe even annoyed, either with himself for not being up to the challenge, or with the world at large for presenting him with the challenge in the first place. Temporary setbacks have left him discouraged. He sees the tunnel but no light at the end of it. If he approached problems in a more positive frame of mind, solutions might be easier to find.

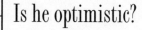

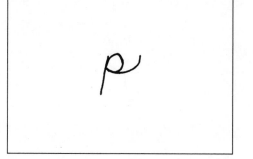

Needs a pep talk sometimes

If you were both crossing a chasm, you'd have to keep on reminding him: "It's going to be okay. Everything will turn out all right in the end. Don't look down." He needs to concentrate on good things coming his way, not on potential problems. Someone should encourage, direct and nurture him. Are you up to that?

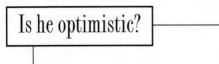

Is he optimistic?

Plays the Blame Game

"Look what I have to deal with!" That could sum up this guy's attitude. There are reasons why he can't be happy, why he doesn't see the bright side, or why he's frustrated about progress. A small part of him enjoys the drama. He may not admit it, but it does. He enjoys finding obstacles and using those as excuses for not being happy.

Not overoptimistic, just turns blind eye to problems (Hope springs eternal.)

 Deep belief in the way things work out, direct actions and responsible reactions, not one for airy-fairy solutions

 Could regard himself as optimist, but falters, picks holes, undoes the good; must think positively

 May have high hopes, but has doubts and reservations; shouldn't take things so seriously

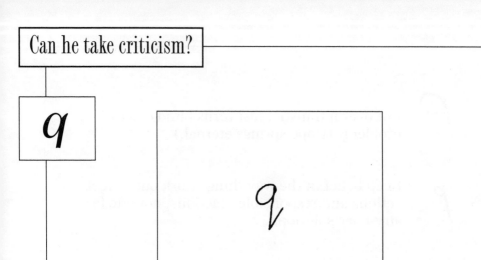

q

Yes, he can—but be polite

This guy will listen to what you have to say about him or his actions, provided your viewpoint is honestly held and kind. But he's sensitive, and will crumble under an all-out attack. Remember, a critique is one thing, lambasting his ideas savagely is quite another. He wants a frank, honest appraisal. Diplomacy will win the day.

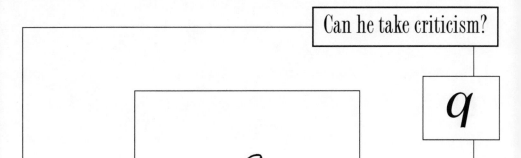

Can he take criticism?

q

Probably not

*The way the **q** leans heavily to the right shows you he backs away from criticism. The more it leans, the more afraid he is of confrontation. Honest opinions may squeak through, but anything more than that could have a negative impact on his confidence. Approach him as you would a small puppy that's just pooped on your new rug. Shouting's not going to help. Be kind.*

q

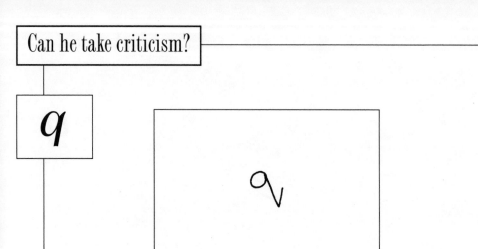

Head to head

When a **q** *tilts to the left, he gives as good as he gets. He comes out of his corner ready to say his piece and lock horns with anyone who takes an opposing viewpoint. He has strong ideas and believes in a vigorous exchange of ideas, preferably resulting in victory to him. Not to be tangled with unless you know what you're doing. Prepare!*

q

Could be secretive

If things go wrong, he may try to blame outside forces. "Oh, that wasn't me—it was him!" He's slow to reveal plans, proposals, problems, thoughts, or feelings until he's sure of the reception they'll receive. The less information you have, the less ammunition you'll have to fire at him, that's what he thinks. And d'you know what? He's right.

q Goes his own way; sharp and impatient; can dole it out but unlikely to handle it himself

Q May slip into defense mode at the first sign of a perceived attack—a tender soul who could be hurt easily and take offense, though he may not appear so

q Agenda bender; may not know where he's coming from; confused by criticism; he likes it that you don't understand him

q Feels like a cog in the machine; maybe has been criticized too much; worn down.

r

Conscientious

Once his head's down and he's involved, he won't be side-tracked easily. He applies himself wholeheartedly when he's interested and no doubt has great follow through. The kind that brings his work home. There are times when he'll be receptive to you, and others when you must stand aside and let him get on with what he has to do.

Is he dedicated?

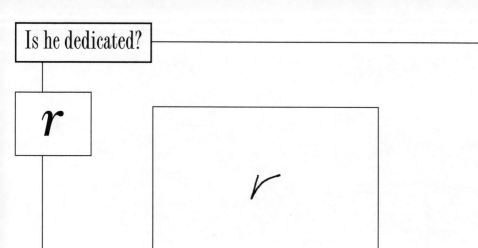

Aware

A nice balance. He takes an interest in the world around him and plays that off against other obligations. It's not to say he can't be conscientious when he wants to be and apply himself to the tasks at hand, just that . . . well, there are many subjects that captivate him. If he confines himself to just one, he might miss out on something.

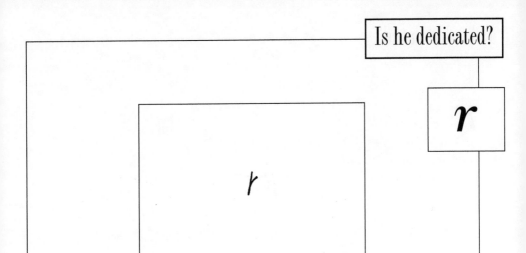

Low-key

May not be the most outgoing or exciting fella you ever met. He keeps a lot of emotion inside, and could be hard to read a lot of the time. Is he working, or just sitting there contemplating the whole idea of getting down to work? What interests him interests him, what doesn't doesn't. Cool, noncommittal, narrow in his interests.

89

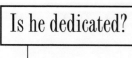

Multi-tasks

*He can watch football, do his taxes, change the baby's diapers, talk to his lawyer on the phone, learn the cello, and play the Lotto, all at the same time, and he'll **still** spot that you forgot to change the bed sheets. He's sharply aware and doesn't miss a trick. Make sure his interest in you is genuine, not just another feather in his cap.*

Always thinking, always occupied, relentless; needs downtime

Wa-a-ay too interested; always trying to find out what's going on; might notice your perfume or remember your anniversary (In other words, a bloodhound.)

Worried; is he doing the right thing? mind spinning off in other directions; you may be way down his list of priorities

"Don't bug me!"—he has an agenda he sticks to; don't intrude; only understands you want attention after you've written it across his pool table with a staple gun

91

S

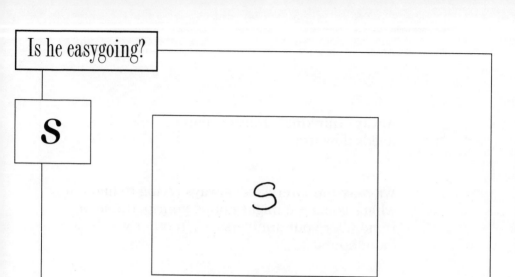

Fairly laid back

*An upright, open **s** tells you he has an easygoing side to his nature. He's ready for anything, doesn't have a fixed point of view, and is certainly not the type to lock horns with people the whole time. If you want to go somewhere, do something, he'll probably tag along. If you want to see a chick flick and he wants to watch football on TV . . . okay, I guess everyone has their limit!*

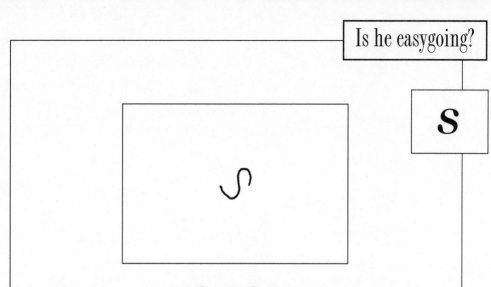

S

The Fighter

He has a point to make and an agenda he wants to see fulfilled. He pushes ahead with it no matter what, determined to bring it to a successful conclusion. Not easily thrown off course, he could be stubborn and even argumentative if you stand in his way or take an opposing viewpoint. Either give in or step aside to let him through.

S

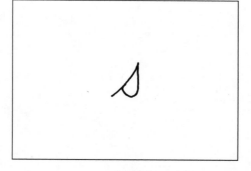

Stern

One of those roll-your-sleeves-up-and-get-down-to-it kind of guys. He probably likes to have his own way, and frowns on those who don't come up to his standard or who question his authority. He won't see it that way himself, of course. But he has very little time for reviewing his own actions—he's too busy supervising yours.

s

Perhaps too easygoing

*The roundness of the **s** indicates that, while he knows what he wants and isn't afraid to push for it, he may be afraid of offending people along the way. This gives him pause for thought. He's considerate and won't deliberately set out to hurt anyone. But don't think he's a pushover. He may be made of sterner stuff.*

Tasks get done in his own way, probably before you know; determined, he won't enjoy being pushed around

Tough cookie; won't welcome interference from you or anyone; control issues dominate (Whatever he's doing, best leave him to it.)

Interested in people—and maybe influencing them; fixed intentions and the will to pursue them; somewhere down the line, may want something from you

Bold, strong, alert, poised for action; may make it himself by stirring things up; doesn't know when enough is enough

t

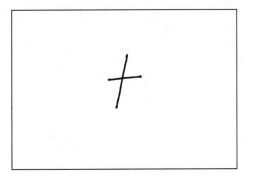

Sincere

*When a **t** is crossed through the center, it means the writer's actions and words come from a good place. Now, having said that, can you trust him with your heart? That's trickier. Sometimes even bad people have a deep conviction that their wrongful actions are justified. So if you're wise, you'll check in with your intuition before making any big moves or taking risks.*

Is he in touch with his feelings?

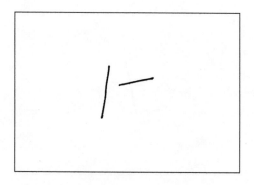

Automatic responses

*The crossbar of the **t** is dislocated. If it doesn't go through the **t**, then the person speaks and acts without considering the consequences. He does what has to be done. He may not mean to hurt you, but he's learned a range of convenient responses that he can fall back on. If he's a soldier or a doctor, that's a good thing. In other cases, it could make him cold, insincere, or even ruthless.*

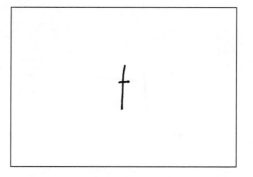

Cool

This kind of person is hard to fathom because he offers so few clues. You may want to feel close to him and be welcomed into his world, but it seems like he can't reveal his true emotions. He's learned to be reserved, keep those emotions under wraps and maybe put on a happy face, while keeping what he really thinks locked inside.

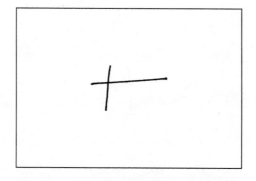

"Everybody listen to me!"

*Could this guy **be** any more out there with what he feels and believes? He expresses himself all the time, even when nobody wants to hear. He seeks to control, guide, direct, oversee everyone and everything in his path. Part of it's because he fears not being in charge; another part's because he compensates for insecurities. You'll need to be just as strong—or silent!*

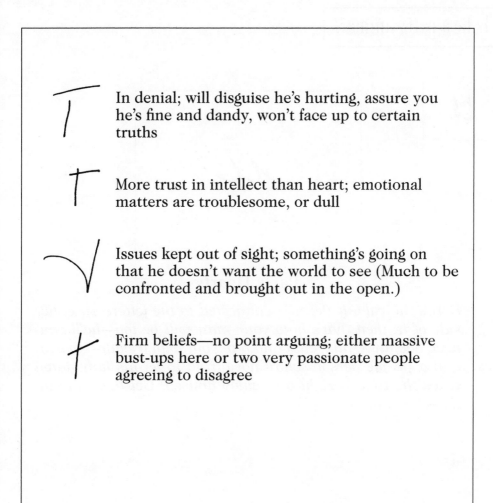

In denial; will disguise he's hurting, assure you he's fine and dandy, won't face up to certain truths

More trust in intellect than heart; emotional matters are troublesome, or dull

Issues kept out of sight; something's going on that he doesn't want the world to see (Much to be confronted and brought out in the open.)

Firm beliefs—no point arguing; either massive bust-ups here or two very passionate people agreeing to disagree

u

Party Hearty

*Here's the rule: If the **u** is connected to the letters on either side of it, then that's how your man will be too—he'll connect. Socialize, mix, chat and hang out with friends—in general a people person who's not afraid to let his hair down when the time is right and enjoy himself. Get those invitations lined up.*

u

U

Fun is a good book . . .

*He'll socialize when he has to, but a **u** that's detached from the letters around it shows that he also loves time alone. He's not afraid of his own company and will happily curl up with a book and his favorite CDs for an evening in. Give him space to breathe. He needs downtime—and that may mean downtime from you too.*

u

u

Selective

This guy doesn't let just anyone join his circle. Only certain people qualify. And he's reluctant to attend every function available. His time is precious and he has to be choosy. He surrounds himself with really close friends, people he trusts and can confide in, and lets the rest go. Once you're in, you're in.

Enjoys many things, all kinds of functions, networking, spreading himself across the social spectrum; may not delve into anything too deeply

Secret issues, private concerns, hidden thoughts and motives; may try too hard and be unintentionally troublesome

Inner tensions; stresses over small matters; spikiness, could be argumentative or controversial at parties (That should break the ice!)

Knows what makes him comfortable and the kind of people he gets along with, and sticks to it; finds it hard to mix with people

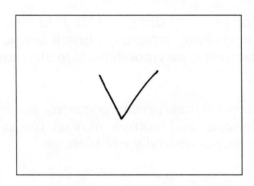

Come and get it!

*By the looks of it, this guy could be pretty unstoppable. When the **v** is large and spread wide like that, his mind is open to all possibilities. He loves being loved. Expect him to enjoy sex in all places and in all its naughty variations. He may not have the same narrow boundaries others have and could be great fun if you get him in the right mood. Lucky you. (Also check his E.)*

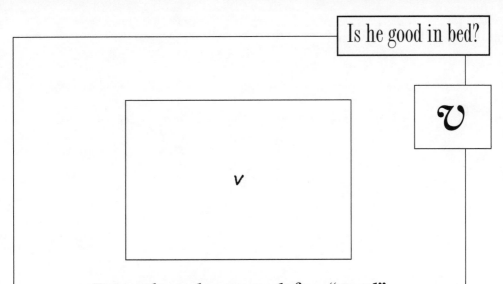

Depends on how you define "good"

*It's all relative, of course. A tiny **v** doesn't mean he has tiny tackle, but it does suggest that what he does with it is a little limited. He has simple and specific tastes and indulges them. He could lack stamina for the long haul, or in extreme cases may be uptight about sex. He'll think he's pretty good, though. So bite your tongue!*

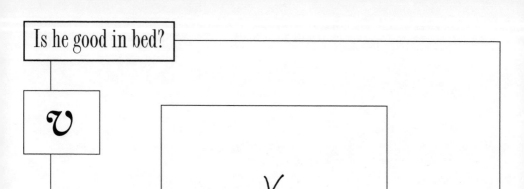

Is he good in bed?

Average

Not too wild, not too conservative, he appears to have a normal sexual appetite. He may be willing to experiment, depending on what the options are, but there's something pretty straight about the way he goes about things. If you're neither excessively shy nor over the top crazy, he'll no doubt satisfy your needs.

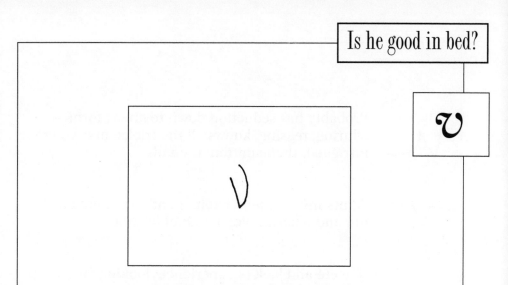

Willing but concerned

There are reservations and worries underlying his approach to sex. Could be that he wants to check you out before becoming too involved; get to know you a little more. Or else he could have germ or intimacy issues. He may be slow to loosen up until you've passed the various checkpoints. Don't rush him.

Probably has seduction down to an art form—
alluring, teasing, knows all the tricks; first you're
intrigued, then smitten, then his

 Wants involvement, excitement; sex should be
fun and pleasurable, not an obligation

 Naïveté and lack of experience; looking for a
mentor, so get ready to show him the ropes
(Respect his charming innocence and try not to
giggle.)

 Not as open as he seems—may be willing, but
torments himself over consequences and issues
of trust (Could be tiresome.)

W

Pretty much

*When all three spikes of the **w** rise to an equal height, the guy has a discerning eye. He knows quality when he sees it and won't settle for anything less. Of course, what's a tasteful piece to one may be junk to another, but basically what we're saying is, he's not the type to gush over trash, or to back a lost cause. I mean, if he were, he wouldn't be with you, would he? Right?*

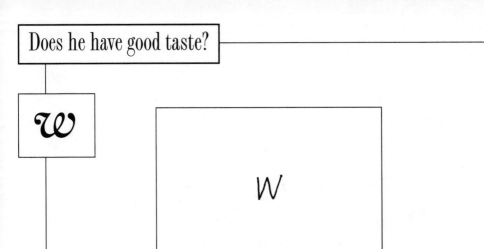

Rigid viewpoint

Tasteful he may be, but he can also be unbending in his views about what is good and what isn't. He sticks to his guns, even if others disagree with him. He thinks he's right, when really it could just be his pride getting in the way, or else he's being difficult and inflexible for the sake of it. This approach could cost him many experiences.

w

W

Please calm down!

He'll probably have enthusiasm for all the wrong things. He simply loves to enjoy life—this person, that person, this vase, that picture-frame, your new rug, the hat you bought last week . . . everything gives him pleasure; he finds it hard to choose between one good thing and the next. Sadly, good taste can't be taught.

Aggressive

He has a winner's mentality and he'll do whatever it takes to come out on top in any situation. If that means being the best at work, that's what he'll do. If that means having the greatest collection of Renaissance paintings in the western hemisphere, then that's what he does. He wants others to think well of him. So he aims high, gives his all to any task, and is determined to make good no matter what.

Won't appreciate criticism of his taste or views—be tactful and keep your opinions to yourself

 Not the kind to enjoy good things alone; to live life to the fullest means sharing it with those he cares about (Nothing wrong there.)

 May have a keen eye and fine taste in chosen areas; tends to be low-key and analytical (Notice that he may have fine things but not tell you he has them.)

Can't be content simply liking something; he has to let you know how much and how expensive it is and how you have to have it too; endless gushing

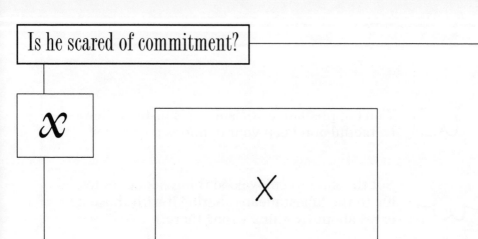

Heart and soul

This guy means business. He's loyal and steadfast, and when he makes promises he tries to keep them. Okay, so maybe he's not totally perfect, but a straight x does indicate a sense of honor, a strong conscience and someone who tries to do the right thing. With those credentials, you can surely forgive him if he falls short now and then.

𝒳

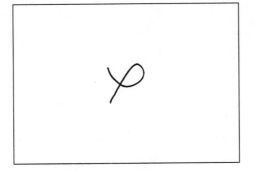

What's commitment?

That loop is not a good sign. It can sometimes mean a man has other fish to fry. Subconsciously, he's not ready to settle down and is in two minds about devoting himself to one person. At the mere mention of weddings and happily ever after, chills run down his spine. If he does commit to one person, he could nevertheless nurse secret thoughts of freedom. You may have to chain him to the altar.

Emotions held inside

*There's an intensity here that suggests intellectual reserve and a low emotional connection, although his commitment may be full and true. Whatever the shape the **x** is (see other pages), if it's very small, then the guy operates within a narrow frame of reference. So he may be very, very, very devoted, or very, very, very distant and aloof. Or both.*

x

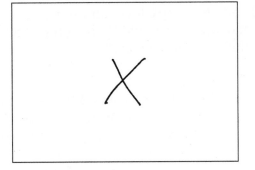

Yours forever more

*The bigger the **x**, the more needy the person will be. He'll give his heart and expect only the best in return. Yet somehow it never works out that way. He often gets hurt. And it's not because people are out to wound him necessarily, more because his heart is so bruised and tender that one unkept promise, one significant letdown, one cold remark may be all it takes to break it.*

Prone to puppy love, an unerring adoration; charming yet naïve (Is he a teenager? If not, what's he playing at?)

 Has reservations; worried he'll get swamped or the rug pulled from under his feet or he'll lose control (Take it slowly, he'll come around, he may be worth it.)

 Gives too much; nothing is too much trouble; you can't repay his devotion, but he wants acceptance and praise

 Great expectations—if you don't meet them or rise to the occasion, he'll tell you (Be sure you know what you're getting into.)

y

A sense of duty

This is the kind of guy tries hard to honor his responsibilities. He actively confronts issues and resolves them. It's even possible that he tries too hard to deal efficiently with everything, perhaps out of fear of being thought weak or ineffectual. But at least he's on top of the game and it's hard to fault him for that.

Is he responsible?

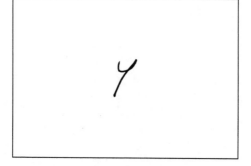

Very dutiful

Here's someone who strives to get things done ahead of time. Bills are paid, deadlines met, promises kept—all, I'm sure, with stunning efficiency. He doesn't like loose ends, or to be thought of as negligent or a slacker. To his mind, confronting a problem is the best way to solve it. Unlikely to shirk responsibilities.

y

Are you talking to me?

*That curlaround tail reveals a fear of blame. He tries hard to overcome problems and leap all of life's hurdles, but creates new problems as he goes. He fears taking responsibility when things go wrong. In fact, he can't believe you're pointing the finger at him. "Me? You're blaming **me** for this mess?" Doesn't want to address his own weaknesses, which may be at the root of any trouble.*

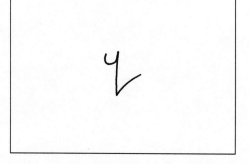

Passes the buck

This guy's not afraid to delegate, and will let others perform tasks that he probably should be handling himself. Some people have a knack of taking on too much then burdening others with the overspill. Often they relinquish that burden so deftly that the recipients don't realize they've been dumped on till it's too late. But this may be the only way he feels he can get things done.

Troubled; many personal issues to resolve; has to open up, face the past, and resolve the problem

 Haunted by unresolved conflicts near the surface; small things—often unrelated—may trigger his unhappiness

 Busy, busy, busy, a never-ending blur of activity; can't really appreciate what he has

 Cheerful excuses, a lot to do, and he's not certain he can manage—should you bail him out? or would it be better if he tried harder?

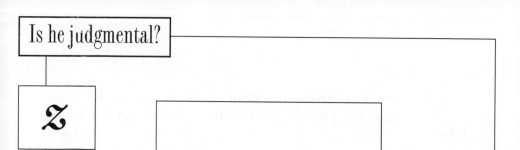

Is he judgmental?

Straightforward critical

He has a point of view and he'll express it. He considers his judgment to be fair and intelligent, and you can probably depend on it. Whether he can take your judgments in return is another matter. Listen to what he says—he sure expects you to—then decide for yourself.

z

z

Eager to say his piece

Here, you're dealing with someone who can't wait to air his opinions. He'll no doubt have a view on your hair, your shoes, how you vote, the car you drive, and back this up with unsolicited advice about how you could make changes or even alter your lifestyle. He means well, but a relationship could feel like hard work at times.

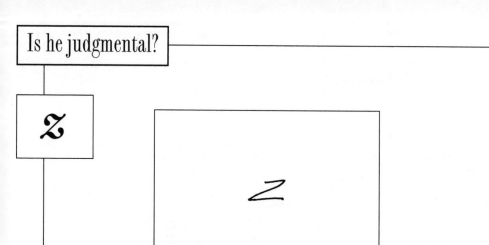

Holds back

Probably because he fears what you will say about him, he tends to stay quiet and observe before rushing to judgment. There's an unwillingness to leap in and open up a can of worms. Better, he thinks, to stay out of the fray, bite his tongue for a while and only speak when he has something to add to the situation.

z

Run for cover

A shrewd and overcritical mind is at work here, which is fine if you get on the right side of him. But if he doesn't like you or the way you do things, he's able to cut you down with his tongue. Very likely he'll have a high opinion of himself and a low opinion of others. Sharp, incisive, opinionated, possibly haughty and self-righteous!

129

2   Held in reserve; you might not know what's going through his mind; he knows more than you think and tells you a lot less

3   Doesn't quite know what to say or where to start; not sure when to speak out or what impact he will have (By the time he decides, may be too late.)

8   Bottled up; speaks only when he's sure he has an accepting audience; you may never learn what he really knows or feels

8   No matter how much he's said, there's always more—but the nitty-gritty problems are concealed from prying eyes

A: Is he self-reliant?

B: Is he a wimp?

C: Does he like to have his own way?

D: Will he try to bully me?

E: Is he horny?

F: Will he communicate his feelings?

G: Does he have experience?

H: Will he appreciate me?

I: Is he set in his ways?

J: Is he possessive?

K: Is he strong?

L: Is he uptight?

M: How does he handle relationships?

N: Does he have a frail manly ego?

O: Does he have a big heart?

P: Is he self-centered?

Q: Is he practical and down to earth?

R: Is he impetuous?

S: Does he walk the talk?

T: Is he a control freak?

U: Does he enjoy life?

V: Does he like being the center of attention?

W: Is he a show-off?

X: Will he overwhelm me?

Y: Does he appreciate the good things in life?

Z: Is he aggressive?

A

Sturdy

A strong, independent A belongs to someone who can go it alone if he has to. There are no fancy strokes, no loops or unnecessary embellishments on it, and that could sum him up too. In an emergency, he will handle it to the very best of his ability. Unlikely to be a shrinking violet, he's used to coping with situations and tackles them head-on.

Is he self-reliant?

A softer touch

Less sure of himself, he doesn't absolutely positively know the right way every time, but he'll do his best. Not the aggressive type. If he appears that way, it's just a defense mechanism. When the A stands apart from other letters, it points to an independent spirit. The closer it gets to other letters, the more reassurance he needs.

A

a

One eye on the past

Here's a guy who gains reassurance from the past—either his own or just the past in general. For some reason he dwells on what has gone before. Maybe it fascinates him, or maybe he reflects on happier times. Or maybe he simply can't escape his past. Whatever the reason, he gains strength from looking back instead of forward.

Strong but stressed

There's inner tension here. Outside obligations or a fear of behaving in certain untried ways weigh on his mind, forcing him into an emotional and mental corner. He may adopt a lofty, "Oh, it doesn't worry me. I'm fine" approach, but in quieter moments he must be aware of the narrowness of the road he's on.

A Not the kind of guy to take control and be in charge unless he has to; somewhat crushed by life, could take years to mature

Determination and drive and more fool you if you get in the way; resolute and tenacious, may stick by a stand even when others say he's wrong

Seems confident, but there's a measure of dependency; he needs approval; a lot more going on than he'd have you believe

Weaker than he'll admit (Sure, he's his own man and says he doesn't need anyone—but he needs help and knows it.)

B

B

What *is* he thinking?

This person does not have a "big" personality. His operations are low-key. He keeps many thoughts and ideas to himself. Don't be deceived, however; there may be an inner grittier determination that's not obvious from the outside. He could succeed by willpower and in small steps rather than by grand gestures.

B

B

Goes for what he wants

A good solid B points to a solid individual who is not afraid to stand up for himself when circumstances call for it. Inwardly he may be quaking, but somehow, when the chips are down, he manages to come up with the goods. He states his case and stands his ground until his needs are met. Not to be messed with.

B

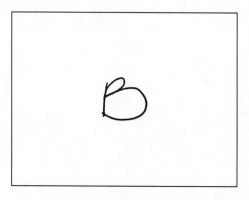

B for Bulldozer

*That bulbous lower half of the **B** drives everything before it. Tactless and insensitive possibly, he rides over obstacles and difficult people to achieve his ends. Ironically, behind this apparent strength lie pockets of weakness, but he's never going to let you see those. His image is one of authority and initiative, and so long as everyone buys into that, how can he lose?*

B

The Ditherer

Needs to be more assertive. He holds back when he should push forward. Something inside—fear, anxiety, self-doubt, apprehension about consequences—prevents him being bold and fighting his corner. Conversely, by taking his time he sometimes gains the advantage over those who rush to pick fights or win small battles. His attitude may actually pay off.

Unafraid to get out there and ask for what he wants (If the B is of medium size, he's shrewd about it. If the B is excessively large, he's more demanding.)

 Not entirely sure if he will get results; he gives it a go anyway (Perhaps he figures if he just keeps on keeping on, he'll come away with *something*.)

 No budging once he's made up his mind; reason goes out the window and pride takes over; often backed into a corner, he doesn't enjoy it

 Anything curling behind the B points to influences from the past he clings to—behavior was programmed

C

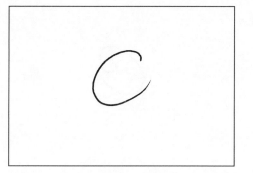

Commanding

The sheer size of the C tells you that the man means business and could swallow you whole. If it's open and unblocked, then he's eager to learn, but in his rush to learn, your needs may get forgotten. Watch out that his apparent confidence isn't just bravado. He wants things his own way, but challenge him and he might just buckle.

Does he like to have his own way?

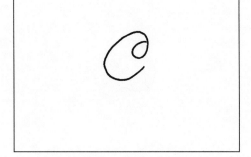

Oh boy—and how!

All too often, this kind of person will declare, "Oh, I'm very flexible and easygoing" when the opposite is true. He holds strong, immovable views on a range of issues, based on hard experience—and in his head that counts for more than any loose talk. So whether it's religion, politics, or whatever else, he'll no doubt insist he's right. Why argue?

C

C

No time for wasters

A thin-C guy knows what's what. He'll sort the wheat from the chaff in no time. He doesn't want to be told anything that doesn't interest him or to spend valuable time dwelling on matters that are not his concern. He's decisive and sticks wherever possible to the relevant, discarding everything else. Now—what was your point?

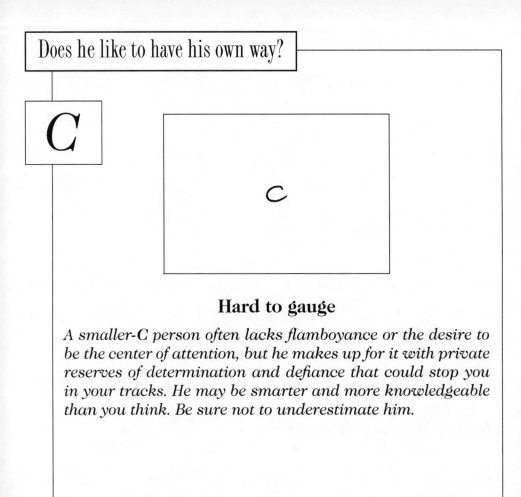

Does he like to have his own way?

C

C

Hard to gauge

A smaller-C person often lacks flamboyance or the desire to be the center of attention, but he makes up for it with private reserves of determination and defiance that could stop you in your tracks. He may be smarter and more knowledgeable than you think. Be sure not to underestimate him.

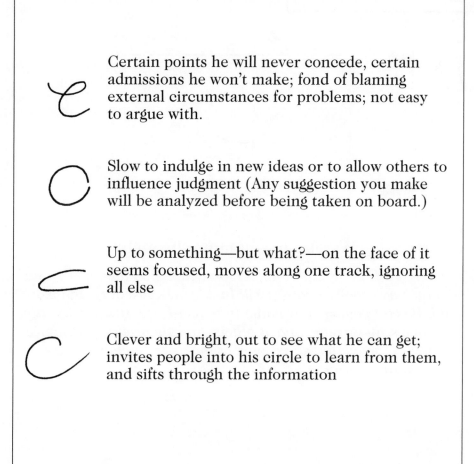

Certain points he will never concede, certain admissions he won't make; fond of blaming external circumstances for problems; not easy to argue with.

Slow to indulge in new ideas or to allow others to influence judgment (Any suggestion you make will be analyzed before being taken on board.)

Up to something—but what?—on the face of it seems focused, moves along one track, ignoring all else

Clever and bright, out to see what he can get; invites people into his circle to learn from them, and sifts through the information

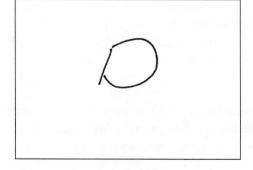

Watch out—coming through!

*When the **D** is big and cumbersome like this, then you stand in the guy's way at your peril. Inside, he's insecure and fearful. He compensates by going into overdrive. His personality becomes his armor, and if others find themselves trampled along the way, that's just part of the deal. Back off, and live to fight another day.*

D

Manageable

There's a balance of force and restraint. He can step up the pace and be strong when he needs to be, but otherwise will conserve his energy. He doesn't need to crush people to get his way. He judges his moment and his approach, aiming to cut a middle path, not too strong, not too weak. Things get done by all kinds of different means.

Will he try to bully me?

D

Please kick me!

He's too timid. Seems to lack the courage of his convictions. Maybe he's scared of comebacks if he asserts himself. In some small way, he reaps benefits from being bullied by people, or at the very least he's so used to it by now that he almost expects to have sand kicked in his face. Everybody's punching bag.

D

)

May appear weak . . .

. . . .*but don't automatically jump to conclusions. He could reach his goals by alternative means. There are unseen reserves. He's learned that sometimes it pays to stay on the sidelines and let the world go by, while observing the activity from afar. He doesn't like to stick his neck out. Nevertheless, he'll only be pushed so far.*

Takes no prisoners; tells what he thinks, and won't let matters rest until he settles the score—hidden power you may not know about until too late

 Fearsome when roused—you may see it as bullying—he's willing to kick butt if he has to; a spark inside, a drive, a motivation that keeps him going

 Overbearing; always on the case, always driving at something, attacking problems, riding over obstacles (Does he ever calm down?)

 Considers actions before he takes them, worries about consequences—an iron fist inside this velvet glove, holding a bunch of flowers

E

Insatiable

*The truth lies in that bottom horizontal bar of the E. If it's un-usually long or if it curves upward, then his libido is proba-bly pumping like a jackhammer. Lust and desire fuse to make him hungry for sex at a moment's notice. I can't vouch for his performance (see **v** for that), but if he's ready and willing, isn't that half the battle?*

Emotional issues

That loop in the center of the E is the product of inner turmoil. Okay, maybe turmoil is too grand a word for it, but he harbors fears and concerns that get in the way of commitment or contentment and which lessen his emotional attachment to people. Even if sex is good, you may feel that you haven't quite made some vital connection with him. Get him to talk about it.

| *E* |

So many thoughts

When the top of the E is overextended, he's thinking and analyzing too much. He's out of balance, using his brain when he should be experiencing a greater emotional or sexual connection. He denies himself the full, rounded human experience by allowing his brain to dominate. He'll be bursting with self-expression, but he may need to ask the Wizard of Oz for a libido.

E

Closed off

He may have a strong sexual appetite, although it could be in short, intense doses. He's quite closed off, so he won't be open to new ideas and fresh ways of doing things. It's the tried and trusted or nothing. There is a lively, youthful soul inside waiting to get out and explore uncharted territories, but it's trapped and it may take more than a couple of dates to release it.

A little inhibited—expect limited emotional and sexual responses; an undercurrent of resistance.

 Holding back (Small **E** people may have a more intense approach to sex, but something is getting in the way—self-doubt or reservations.)

 Emotional and sexual requirements are greater than they seem; takes a lot to fulfill him; good sex needs to be backed up by feelings and exploration

 Feels undervalued, not having needs met; a sense of undeserving, and unworthiness for love and gratification

Will he communicate his feelings?

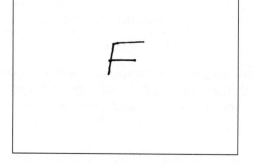

Strong, rigid

Good for frank discussions. He faces issues head-on, appraises them, thinks around them, then delivers his opinion. He communicates because he sees no sense in holding back. Not the type to turn away when his voice needs to be heard, he'll enjoy participating in open discussions and using his intellect to solve problems, even emotional ones. He may not be as sensitive as he could be.

F

Know it all

He may discuss, and he may appear to listen, but in the end he'll want his views to win out. There's a control element to his communication. He needs to feel you're in tune with him. Up to a point he'll do it with an open mind, but after that, you'll be expected to weigh in on his side. Big on expressing views, low on emotional involvement.

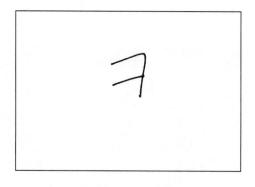

Hard to read

In times of conflict or direct communication he seems to be more in touch with the past than the present. Today's actions are based on leftover emotional distractions of yesterday. He tries to fend off people's approaches by turning away and going inside himself. Instead of speaking out, he holds back. Nice, but hard to pin down.

F

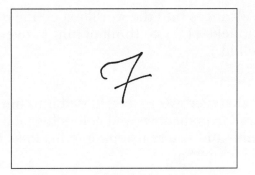

Hurt

He could take every opportunity to be offended or to play your emotions like a violin. He's prone to deep bouts of self-pity and is beset with "Nobody understands me" moods. But maybe nobody understands him because he's not being honest about the real problem. He requires a patient audience and a sharp reminder that your relationship is not all about him.

Advances into the world expecting to be attacked (Try to think of him as oversensitive child.)

Whatever was indoctrinated into him as a child still overshadows and colors his views—listen to him and you're listening to his folks (He's probably unaware.)

Likes to oversee, without direct involvement—this intellectual, aloof approach could divorce him from life

Not the best communicator—small **F** people keep a lot inside and let only the essentials out; secretive and mysterious

G

Ready to go

*An open, unobstructed **G** tells you he has an appetite for new things, even a taste for adventure—a trip to the Pyramids, ballooning across Africa—or maybe he just likes dining in the hottest new restaurants. Whatever his fancy, he'll go for it in a big way. He loves trying different experiences, and the wider and looser the "mouth" of the **G** is, the truer this is likely to be.*

G

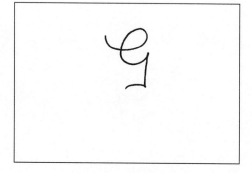

Limited horizons

The loop tells you he's been around long enough to know that if you stick your tongue in an electric light socket, you're going to get hurt—and he doesn't want to get hurt again. Today, certain areas are off-limits. He doesn't want to go there, so don't try to make him.

G

Blocked

Fear leads him to cut off his supply of good. He stands in his own light. Whatever he's been through in life, it has left him wary of biting off more than he can chew. Now he is careful and dismissive of opportunities. They must fit his needs exactly or he won't participate. Needs to open up a little more. Life is for living.

G

Choosy

He wants to learn, wants to cast his net wider, but he spends too much time scrutinizing the options. It's possible he's very busy, so he needs to be picky. If he's just being overzealous, though, he should snap out of it. You can't have everything in life, but if you don't make important decisions, sometimes you end up with nothing.

Been there, bought the T-shirt—almost defiant resistance to change; likes to have a good time, but in his own way, when he's good and ready

Lacking in curiosity; could have one interest he pursues to the exclusion of all else; sees no reason to do things he doesn't like

Dull or just selective?—a limited-horizon guy who could be difficult to reach

Endless reasons for not participating or venturing outside his comfort zone; sees only the pain and not the gain

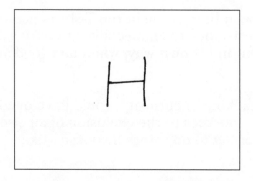

Love and cherish

This guy probably has his head screwed on when it comes to relationships. It's impossible to say he'll never take you for granted, but he is seeking balance and mutuality with give and take on both sides. There is a strong connection and even respect here that could make for a solid, ongoing partnership. Who could ask for anything more?

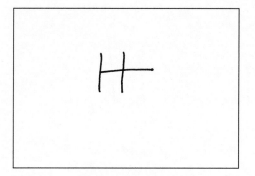

Comes on strong

That overbearing cross-bar could spoil everything. He can't keep his feelings in. He wants control, and insists that his point of view dominates. All of which is fine if you like to be dominated and play second fiddle. Just remember, if you give in once you could be setting a precedent for all time.

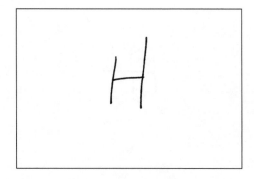

Hero worship

*When the right side of the **H** is tall, it means the guy idolizes his partner and is devoted. Once he has found you, he won't want to let you go. No request is too great, no wish too ridiculous to be granted. Well, okay, maybe he's not a **total** pushover, but he'll do his best to satisfy your needs. Could be a little over the top, though.*

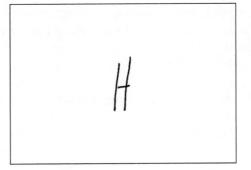

Up close and personal

A squished H means the relationship could either be snug or even suffocating—depends on how you feel about closeness. He'll be there at your side like a faithful puppy. What he's looking for is literally his other half, the side of him that completes the whole. If you're that person, the two of you will be inseparable. Is that what you want?

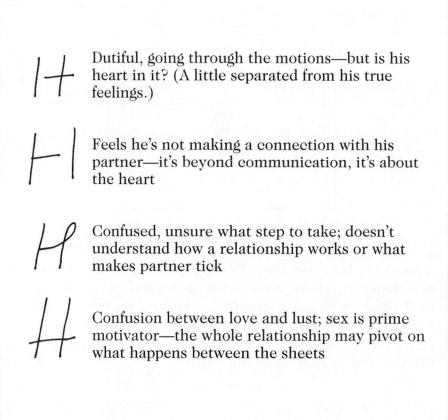

Dutiful, going through the motions—but is his heart in it? (A little separated from his true feelings.)

Feels he's not making a connection with his partner—it's beyond communication, it's about the heart

Confused, unsure what step to take; doesn't understand how a relationship works or what makes partner tick

Confusion between love and lust; sex is prime motivator—the whole relationship may pivot on what happens between the sheets

I

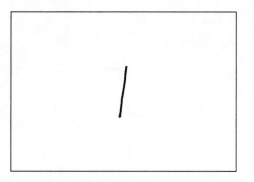

Free flowing

This guy is very independent and won't want to be pinned down. (If the I is distanced from the words around it, this is especially true. When it's squeezed between other words, he's more dependent.) He is not overly committed to any particular view or lifestyle or approach, but wants to be free to explore and grow as much as possible.

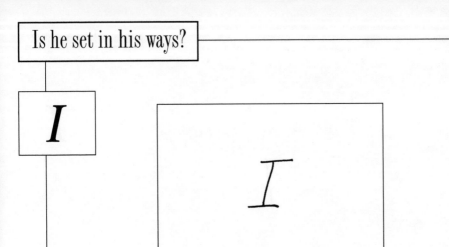

Comfort zone

He knows what he likes and he sticks to it. In fact, his whole life involves sticking to the tried and tested. If it's new and dangerous, he'll simply retire to his nest and wait until the challenge has passed. It's not that he's afraid, simply that he sees no reason to go in search of fresh horizons when he has everything he likes right here.

I

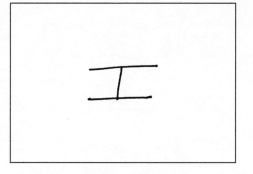

Control freak

*Does this guy ever leave the house? He likes to be in control, to have a finger in every pie, just to make sure it all goes well and is to his liking. Instead of enjoying an expansive life based on freedom and self-expression, he hems himself in with rules and barriers and by trying to be on the case the whole time. He needs to let go—**big-time!***

175

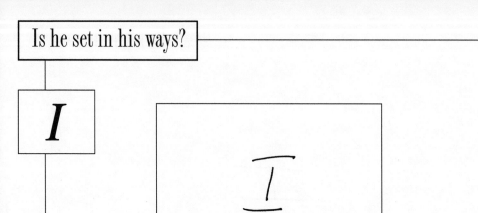

Loosening up

His approach is a nice blend of flying free and staying close to what he knows. In other words, he steers a middle course—fixed in some ways, open and adaptable in others. So long as the two of you agree on what should be fixed and what is up for negotiation, you could be set for a good time. But can you agree? That's the question.

176

Hard to please; a lot of things are set in stone; protective (Win his trust first, coax him out of his shell, and then you can start transforming him.)

 The past won't go away—the trailing loop behind the **I** tells that (The bigger the loop, the more emotional baggage.)

 Dynamic; a man who flies by the seat of his pants (Might be fun to watch what happens next.)

 On the road to somewhere, handling whatever happens as best he can; a measure of stability others don't have, not easily crushed by adversity

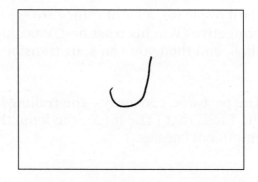

The People Person

He is free and easy with friendships. They come, they go. He loves having his buddies around, but it never becomes too suffocating. Everything is kept light and superficial. Without attachments, he would be lonely, so he keeps it flowing. But he may be difficult to get a grip on. You think he's into you, but are you just one of a thousand he's hanging out with? You'll never be sure.

J

Attached

There's method in his madness. Once you swim into his waters, it may be difficult to find your way out again. Nothing sinister maybe, but he likes to keep certain people close. It's tough knowing whom to trust, so he only lets certain people in and, once hooked, they may not want to leave. This includes you. There is a way out if you want it, but do you really want it?

J

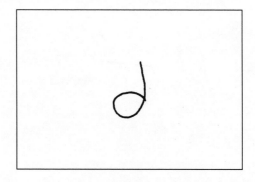

In with the in crowd

He has two sets of people in his life—an inner circle of trusted friends, then everyone else. That loop points to a select band of confidantes. The bigger the loop, the bigger the band. If you're in, then he won't want you to leave, and you're unlikely to want to escape. The rest of the world can do its worst, but if he has his pals around him he feels secure.

Compartments

Different kinds of people mean different things to him, and he may well keep one faction entirely separate from the other. This is because there's a clear division within him, the public self versus the private self, and something—a sense of self-preservation maybe—urges him to maintain a distance between the two sides. Which one are you on?

Needy, craves friendships, needs reassurance and support; treasures longtime friends like precious metals

 Very few admitted to his inner sanctum—there's a fear of exposure and allowing too many strangers in

 Dark currents of insecurity swirl around him, doesn't feel worthy of committed friendships—if you become too close, he will fear losing you

 Loyal to those he invests time in (A part of him wants to hold back. Be glad to spend time with him, but don't try to own him.)

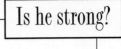
K

Strong-arm tactics

That extra-long upper arm of the K points to a forceful character who doesn't like to hear the word no. The guy wants his own way and he's not afraid to crack the whip in order to get it. He may drive a hard bargain. In some cases, you may even get the feeling that he could use his authority against you if you don't toe the line. Then again, perhaps he's all talk—you never know.

Strong but caring

His neediness overrides any drive he may have to bully people. He prefers a personal connection, physical contact, and acceptance, and will probably go to great pains to achieve personal endorsement from others. He may come on a little strong sometimes, but if you value and respect him, he will respond in kind.

K

Guards his heart

He takes a bold stand and puts on the face of authority in order to convince others that everything's okay and all parts are working, but underneath he's suspicious, cautious, slightly troubled by those who would befriend him too easily. You might never get truly close to him, because he doesn't feel okay about himself.

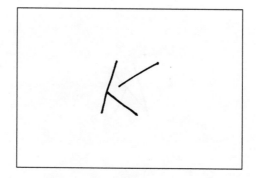

Sugarcoated

What seems like charming behavior at first could prove to be otherwise over time. Behind that façade lies an altogether more ruthless streak. He may not be malicious but he's not afraid to bring pressure to bear on others when he needs to achieve certain ends. Don't get suckered in by appearances. He means business.

Manipulative?—not fully in touch with his feelings or maybe even his conscience; not a bad person, but may need saving from himself at times

 Undermined by self-doubt—might seem firm and sure of what he wants, but he's not; any apparent strength is to compensate for a sense of inadequacy

 Uses every trick and method to ensure others give what he wants; charming, persuasive, or mildly aggressive—do you have the guts to stand up to him?

 Not one to leave people guessing (Intentions are probably honorable, but could be difficult, especially if you have a mind of your own.)

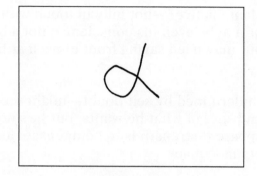

Inhibitions

Certain topics or experiences—probably of a sexual nature—remain taboo. He appears to be suppressing a deep well of anxieties, doubts, or fears. Maybe he was raised with strict beliefs and is slowly breaking them down. If so, there is still a long way to go. The smaller the loop, the fewer inhibitions there are.

L

Straightforward

If there are taboos, they're few and far between and he's working through them. The tendency here is to be open-minded and take life as it comes. If he doesn't share another person's views, that's fine. He may not agree with them, but does he have to? He believes in "live and let live," and that has to be a good thing.

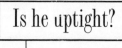

Is he uptight?

L

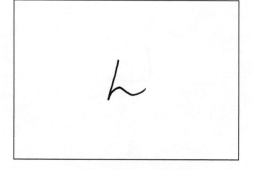

A little troubled

Certain matters are too near the knuckle. He's not comfortable with them and flinches inwardly when conversation turns to these subjects. He's a little uptight and if you don't want to offend him you should tread warily. Having said that, it's unlikely anything will trouble him so deeply that it wrecks his entire day.

L

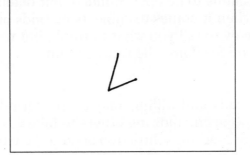

Apprehensive

If you plan to deal with delicate issues, you'd be wise to start slowly and work up from there. Certain topics of conversation are considered danger zones and you could trigger alarm bells if you don't take into account his sensibilities. He's cautious, and may not be as open-minded as you are—take it easy.

Claims to be open-minded, but defenses are up when it comes to subjects he finds offensive; not slow to tell you what to think, but won't thank you for doing the same to him

Ready and willing, may even overindulge and be too open, allowing others to take advantage (Something a little too good to be true here.)

May not be inhibited, but there's a limit to how much he wants to know (Not exactly a firecracker.)

Blatant sex is a no-fly zone—this guy believes one shouldn't be talking openly about sexual matters or delving into other taboo areas

M

Controlling

He hasn't developed a sufficient sense of ease yet to be able to let go and allow emotional matters to take their own course. There have to be rules. Things ought to be done a certain way. Usually, the angular M points to someone who's mature in more practical ways, but tries to impose that same practicality on relationships. You may have to compromise a lot.

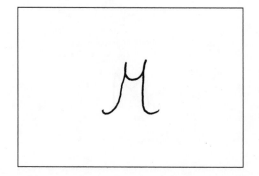

Controlling, but with style

The spikes denote a sharp, almost idealistic view of relationships that expects certain standards or principles to be adhered to for the purpose of show. So marriage becomes a performance for the benefit of the rest of the world, but internally expect stresses from keeping up this façade. It's easy to say "just relax," but harder to do.

M

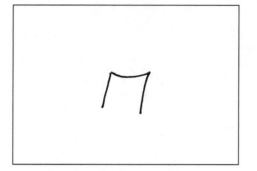

Lacking in deeper feelings

When the M looks more like a tunnel entrance, he would prefer a friend to a lover. If you're both working by the same rule book and you have interests in common, then this should work well. But if you're into deep and meaningful, and real feelings matter to you, then this may not be the guy for you. He probably puts his career or hobbies ahead of lovey-dovey stuff.

Strong and protective

There's a maturity and softness here that promise an interesting relationship, and hopefully a longstanding one filled with balance and mutual love. He needs a lover, a pal, and a champion. Loyalty is important, because he sees relationships as a chance to advance through life together, one solid unit against the rest of the world. If you share that vision—bingo!

More likely attached to parental teachings than an old lover, but whatever went on is still being retained; sees these influences as a mainstay of his life

 Nothing you say or do will really ever be good enough—his expectations are too high (Standards probably set by his mother.)

 A guy with a strong personality and his own life to lead; he needs someone with an independent nature and an agenda separate from his own

 "Hands off—she's mine!"—he nurtures and guards the relationship jealously; a sturdy guardian, someone to watch over you (Is that what you asked for?)

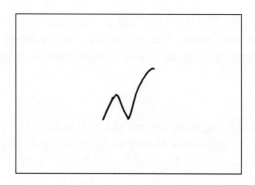

"Don't hit me"

One wrong word to this guy and he'll be crushed. It could be that his parents were rough on him as a kid, or he just realizes he has certain vulnerabilities. He can't take criticism, perceiving it as an assault on his manhood, and the taller that right-hand arm stretches up, the more pronounced this will be. He's terrified of being seen to fail, so he'll try that much harder to please you.

N

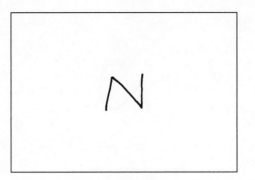

Solid, secure

He won't appreciate unwarranted attacks, but if the criticism is genuine and helps him understand himself better, he'll take it on board. He wants to be strong for himself as well as others. His resolve is unshakable, his will to serve genuine. Setbacks are viewed as temporary, obstacles as bumps in the road. We should all have at least one person like this in our life.

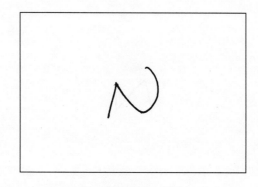

Terrified of attack

Look at the protective arm on that thing! He comes out of his corner fighting. Everyone thinks he's strong because that's the image he gives off. In reality he's as weak as a newborn lamb and scared of being found out or taken to task over mistakes. And because he never knows from which direction attacks will come, he's constantly on guard. A brittle ego. Argumentative.

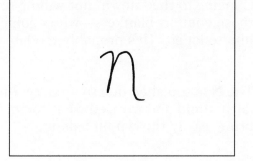

N

Composed

He's a mix of weak and strong. This person can be knocked down, but he takes reasonable steps to protect his private self and his feelings, and conducts himself with a certain amount of dignity, hoping to avoid attacks. It's a ploy that works. But sometimes the world doesn't play the game by our rules, and if you push him too far he could crumble quite quickly.

Clinging to the known, not willing to release those comfort blankets—who's going to persuade him to let go? (It's probably too late.)

The **N** is squished due to anxiety; this person is fairly timid and worried what tomorrow will bring; easily thrown off balance

Long way to go before he is mature enough to deal with the world normally; lacks flexibility and openness—could be dull and uninspiring for anyone dating him

 Not fully in control of his life or emotions; could be hurt deeply; possible that at some level he draws pleasure from the pain and welcomes abuse

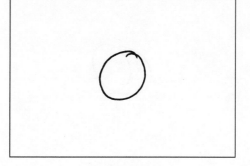

Bull's-eye

An oversized, rounded O often goes with a big heart. Usually, you're looking at someone who has been hurt a whole lot, sometimes even torn apart. Because of this he is able to feel other people's pain. He's sympathetic to the plight of those who are suffering or in trouble. Externally strong; internally soft.

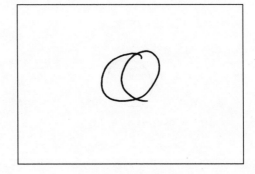

Divided loyalties

He's in two minds. Half of him wants to give, give, give, the other half is less inclined to participate, and it's this conflict that often proves so puzzling to others. The outer appearance of benevolent authority is contradicted by a murkier side, one that doesn't trust people as much as it should, and which has learned to hold back rather than risk being too vulnerable.

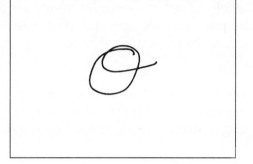

O

What lies beneath

*Answer: A lot lies beneath. Hidden depths, feelings of uncertainty, distrust and even anxiety—things he may never allow you to see. When the **O** is divided in this way, so are his emotions. He has learned not to open up unnecessarily, in case he gets exploited. But what's the cost? He feels distant at times and misunderstood.*

Reaching out to be understood, yet dealing with the past; unsure how much of true self to show people, but learning slowly

Small **o** may be unyielding, but could be generous in the right circumstances; probably thinks around the subject before giving of himself

A little wary; prior to any open display of feelings, wonders if it will go well; slow in coming forward (But bear with him—he'll shine in the end.)

Many pressures bear down on this guy—he tries to remain above it all and be true to his heart, but it's difficult; needs to focus more on his own needs

P

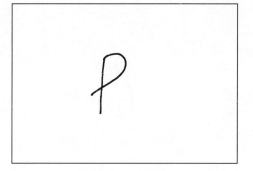

Not interested

If it doesn't directly concern him, he doesn't want to know. His field of interest is narrow and that's just how he likes it. If you're not talking about issues that affect his life in some way, he'll turn off and think about something else. An irritating trait perhaps, but good if you don't want to waste time on irrelevancies.

P

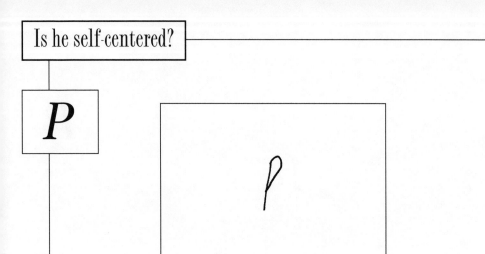

The Snob

He has very little time for those who don't measure up to his personal standards. He lives in a world of his own creation and rarely looks over the fence into anyone else's. Furthermore, he believes that the air on his side is better; his friends are of a superior quality, his tastes are simply the best. If you don't happen to agree, you may find his company annoying.

Nice balance

*A well-proportioned **P** points to a person who shows interest in matters beyond his own personal affairs. He is willing to share the spotlight and probably has many topics he can discuss. He's curious about the wider world and knows what's going on. Perceptive, aware, and a good listener. Bravo!*

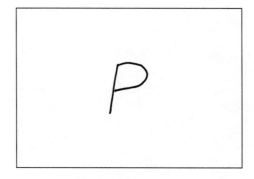

Nosy neighbor

This guy is interested in anything and everything. His telephone is Gossip Central. Nothing escapes his eyes or ears. His antenna is constantly raised and his receiver switched on. He loves to hear about you and what you have to say. Equally, he loves to hear what you have to say about others. Keep it interesting—NEVER be dull.

Interest in the world extends to about six inches away from his face; baffled by a lot of what goes on around him and shows little concern

 Tainted by his upbringing; something is holding him back; yearns to get out there and be part of the crowd

 A hunter, and his prey is information that could be used against you at a later date (He knows more than you think.)

 Emotional overdrive; he could know everything and still not be satisfied—does he fear friends and colleagues are conspiring against him?

Is he practical and down to earth?

Q

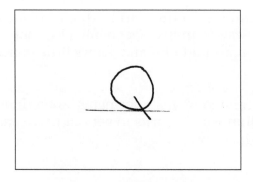

Laying it on the line

If the Q sits on the line, then the guy will probably have his act together in many key ways. Of course, his idea of having his act together may not be anyone else's, but through it all there's likely to be a certain pragmatism and knowingness underscoring his actions. The larger the Q, the more overbearing he's likely to be with it.

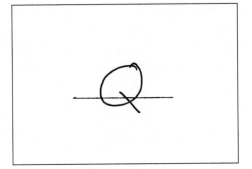

Mired in detail

*The **Q**'s below the line—that's telling you that the guy tends to take on too much and gets swamped by tasks and responsibilities. He tackles life in a serious, committed way, with the result that issues weigh heavily on his mind. Right now, the world seems to be controlling him instead of the other way round.*

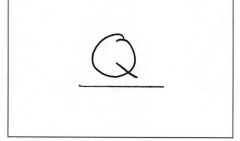

Losing touch

A dreamer, someone who may not lay adequate foundations beneath his plans. He tackles tasks either in half-hearted ways, hoping that someone else will pick up the pieces later, or in impractical ways without fully thinking them through. He needs grounding, and should apply his mind to the whole process, not just the fun parts.

Q

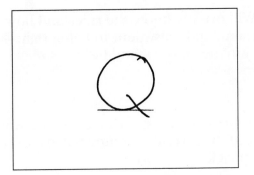

Overbearing

Too often, large-Q people have a tendency to push their views onto others. They have something to say and they believe it's right, so why shouldn't everyone else hear it? This person sees himself as having a natural authority or important knowledge and could lay these on people without caring how they might be received.

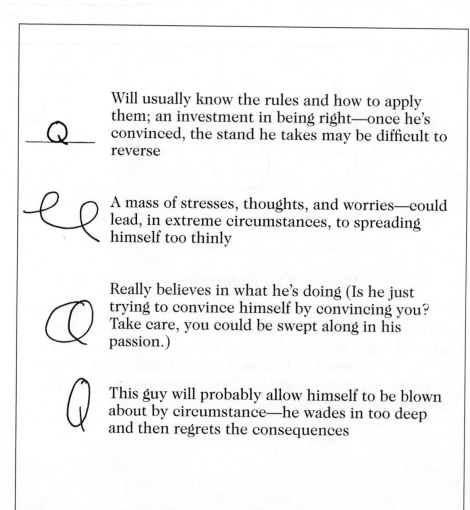

_Q_

Will usually know the rules and how to apply them; an investment in being right—once he's convinced, the stand he takes may be difficult to reverse

A mass of stresses, thoughts, and worries—could lead, in extreme circumstances, to spreading himself too thinly

Really believes in what he's doing (Is he just trying to convince himself by convincing you? Take care, you could be swept along in his passion.)

This guy will probably allow himself to be blown about by circumstance—he wades in too deep and then regrets the consequences

R

Flies by the seat of his pants

Not much lofty preparation goes into this guy's affairs. Or if it does, he's a whiz at making it seem like he's doing none at all. He tackles tasks on the fly, thinks as he goes, handles problems and overcomes obstacles spontaneously. He believes that too much planning dulls the brain. Far better to dive in, get your hands dirty and see what happens.

Sees all, knows all

He likes to look ahead, viewing problems before they happen. He's a planner. He wants to know his options ahead of time so that he can make the best choices. The cautious type, he will be reluctant to leave things to chance if that can be avoided. More likely to ask questions, make to-do lists, and keep people on their toes.

R

Held back by worries

It's as if the guy is wearing a backpack of concerns, and he refers to these before he takes action. A lot of factors are weighed up. He probably wishes he were more impetuous, and he may well cut loose on occasion, but usually it's when he's sure of his ground. If not, he could question endlessly what needs to be done and create confusion where there shouldn't be any.

R

Fired up and ready to go

Perhaps he had go-ahead parents who didn't let him relax as a kid, because now he's up and at 'em the whole time. He works hard to make sure things go well, but in his view just getting in there and taking action is half the task. He still references thinking and approaches imposed on him as a child. But if they work, why challenge them?

R Happy with the tried and trusted, rarely strikes out impulsively; more likely a follower than a leader

R Works to his own agenda—you may not be dealing with a ball of fire here, yet slow and determined can win the race (Remember the tortoise and hare.)

 Gathers, observes, surveys; thinks on behalf of others and leads his troops from the front; nothing left to chance

 Makes plans, takes actions, follows convictions; strong, bold; others' opinions have little bearing on his decisions, but their mistakes do; his own man

S

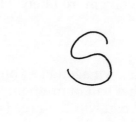

All for show

A super-sized S that overwhelms the small letters around it is a sure sign that the guy is not all he portrays himself to be. On the surface, sure, he seems outgoing, bold, strong, and go-ahead, but it's a performance. Underneath lurks a quieter soul who feels he needs to wear many masks to get through the day. If you can't cut through to the real person, he could be a bit hard to handle.

S

His own person

He makes the rules. He won't go down any path until he's sure where it's taking him. If he seems headstrong and commanding, that's because he is. Willful, rigid in his outlook, and unable to bend as circumstances dictate. Could be a hard case who thinks he's acting in everyone's best interests when he may not always be.

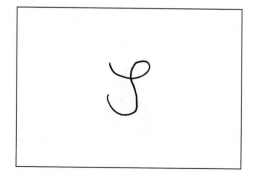

The blinders are on

*He approaches life with certain attitudes firmly in place. He'll tell you exactly what he thinks, but is it **really** what he thinks or what he's been conditioned to think? His defenses are up and he's watching his back, afraid that others will put one over on him. Too much mental clutter gets in the way of reasoned approaches.*

S

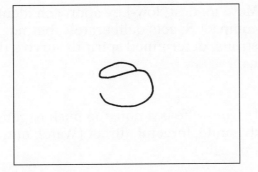

Head in the sand

He takes too much for granted, moving through life without fully thinking through the consequences. He could neglect to say or do the right thing when it really counts, making difficult problems worse, or he may ride roughshod over obstacles and opponents, expecting problems to take care of themselves.

S   More modest, low-key approach identified by a compact **S**; acts deliberately, but not with force; strong, determined spirit to survive the long haul

S   Driven—life is a nonstop push to get things done; dynamic, forceful, direct (Watch out, he's coming through.)

S   Moves swiftly through situations with his head full of thoughts—these he may or may not share with you—he's on the case, doing what has to be done

S   Some issues won't be compromised (When his mind's made up, dissent's a waste of breath. Don't try.)

T

The Overseer

*When the crossbar of the **T** extends to the right, it's a sign of someone with control issues. He likes to make sure things go right and in a way that meets his standards. He may not bully you into conforming to his demands, but you'll be made all too aware of what those demands are. There may be friction if you don't comply.*

T

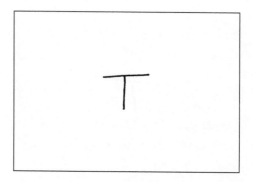

Evenhanded

Firm in his own mind about what is important and what's not, he doesn't feel the need to influence others unduly. He sets an example for others to follow. If they do, fine. If not, that's their problem. There's a balance and inner strength here that's quite admirable but difficult to attain. You either have it or you don't, and he has it in spades.

T

The Ultra–Control Freak

He'd be busy plotting to take over the world if he weren't so involved in controlling everything else around. He's caught up in life's minutiae and loves to interfere. Some internal drive causes him to seek to manipulate circumstances and maneuver people to suit his scheme of things. Good if you need someone to relieve you of a burden; tough if you like to have a say in your own life.

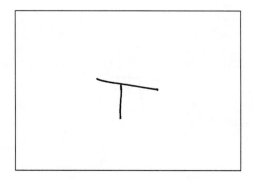

Accommodating

At the back of his personality is a desire to oblige others and maybe even teach them a thing or two about life, using his own standards as an example. He bends in the prevailing wind of opinion, listening to people and taking their views on board before acting. But don't confuse this for weakness, because he may be smarter than he looks.

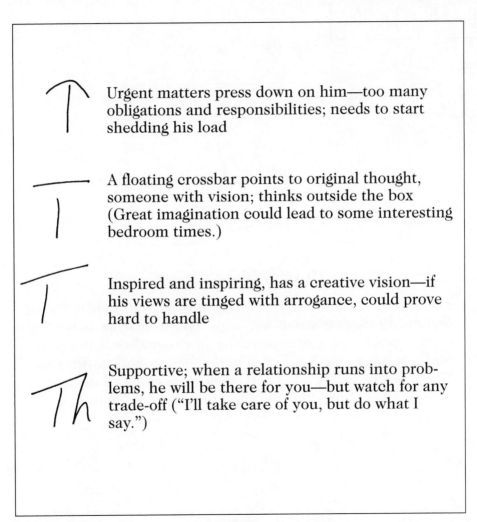

Urgent matters press down on him—too many obligations and responsibilities; needs to start shedding his load

A floating crossbar points to original thought, someone with vision; thinks outside the box (Great imagination could lead to some interesting bedroom times.)

Inspired and inspiring, has a creative vision—if his views are tinged with arrogance, could prove hard to handle

Supportive; when a relationship runs into problems, he will be there for you—but watch for any trade-off ("I'll take care of you, but do what I say.")

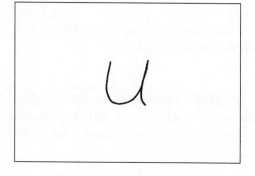

Hungry like the wolf

*The stronger, bolder, and wider the **U**, the more he devours opportunities that come his way. Think of it as a pair of arms reaching upward, drawing in experience, enjoyment, and whatever else it takes to make for a rounded, fun time. That's not to say he's not choosy or discerning in his tastes, just that he's more likely to play the game of life in a wider arena.*

U

Reservations

*The loop highlights either a pocket of doubts or a reluctance to participate freely unless he feels he's considered the consequences beforehand. Not every offer he's presented with gets through the net. Indeed, some will positively turn him off. He worries more than most and functions in a narrower sphere. Is that a good thing? Depends what kind of **U you** have.*

Does he enjoy life?

$$\mu$$

Selective

Choices are made, preconceptions and prejudices adhered to. He has a specialized appetite and tends to filter out a lot of experiences before he really knows what they entail. In that way, he could be his own worst enemy. A narrow existence can be limiting. Maybe he needs to widen his scope, take more calculated risks, live bigger.

Likes to sample broad spectrum of events and interests; flits from one place and one group to another; misses out on many good things

Influences from the past play a huge part—afraid to let go of what once was (Time to cut away any dead wood.)

Narrow frame of reference, limited choices—opportunities may pass him by and he won't even know; playing safe means not exposing himself to hurt

Maybe life has taught him being too impulsive does no good; or he's had his fill of trying to get somewhere and life's injustices; reluctant to participate

Does he like being the center of attention?

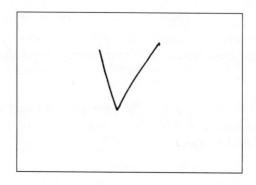

"Look who just walked in—it's me!"

A super-sized V belongs to someone who makes an impact wherever he goes. You certainly know when he's in the room. He's likely to be opinionated, if not downright boisterous, naturally commanding attention. His joie de vivre makes him fun to be with, if a tad unpredictable.

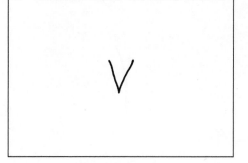

Composed

The type who'll shine when he needs to but otherwise remains in the background. He lacks the urge to play to the gallery the whole time. Something inside of him holds energy in reserve. He can be withdrawn and go unnoticed if he so chooses, or impose his authority if he feels his purpose would be better served that way.

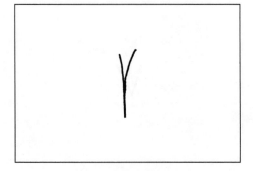

Untouchable

There are parts of him that remain secret. He nurses deep anxieties about how he will be viewed and received by others, and so he plays a game, leaving everyone guessing as to what's really going on. Socially, he'll be agreeable and even tantalizing, but won't want to go out on a limb. He will want to be portrayed in the best light.

V

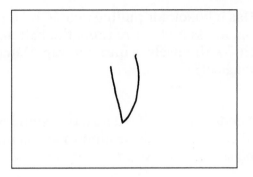

Protective

He shies away from others, and although he may seek attention, when the spotlight shines on him he doesn't quite know what to do next. He plays hard to get, recoils from those who would probe deeper than he's comfortable with, and generally refuses to act out any role other than the ones he chooses for himself. Mysterious and coy.

Has a knack for pulling people in, a natural openness and allure (Sets the bait and people throw themselves into his trap. Dangerous or magical?)

 Needs support of friends; can stand alone, but likes to have pals around to act as buffer (Don't be surprised if you're invited as moral support.)

 A level of confusion and self-doubt regarding the impression he might make; impulses get quashed; undermined by hesitation and self-questioning

 Looking for him in the limelight is like playing "Where's Waldo?"—feels embarrassed when all eyes turn on him; would rather let someone else be the focus

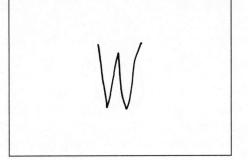

"Look what I can do!"

An oversized W points to a need to be recognized by others and admired for personal achievements. And this person will probably have lots of solid achievements worth bragging about. He is not afraid to be bold and to stand out from the crowd, but there are control issues. He will take an uncompromising stand at times when maybe he should be backing down.

"Hey—I'm over here, guys!"

This large W tells you the guy has a deep need to make his mark and to receive public endorsement for it. His demands for attention will be tempered by humility and an appreciation that others deserve their own moment in the sun too. In fact, this mix could seem quite charming.

W

W

Doing what comes naturally

A small, pointy W denotes a more modest, restrained individual. He may have plenty to say, and many significant achievements to his credit, yet he can't bring himself to make a song and dance about them. It's enough that he tries hard and does well. The reward comes in completing the task to a high standard. Everything above that is icing on the cake.

Pleasantly humble

If this guy has achievements worth crowing about, he no doubt lacks the desire to plaster his success across bill-boards. Let others say how great he is, he's happy just going about his business uninterrupted. That lack of drive can often mean that he fails to make adequate strides toward his goals. It's possible to be too humble.

Would make a good lawyer—will respond to any perceived attack with a level of outrage and hurt that seems disproportionate; a need to come out on top always

 This guy's desire for greater recognition is pegged down by others' influence; friends and family bring reason or caution to bear when whims could lead him astray

 Seeks to impress and open up to outside influences; maybe needs a pat on the back for even minor accomplishments—"Is that good? Did I do well?"

 An inflated sense of pride; will like to show off at every opportunity (Getting to the real person could be difficult—his stories may be exaggerated.)

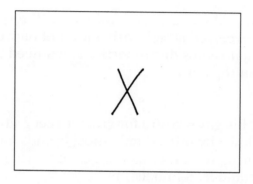

Power sharing

He is looking for mutuality within the relationship. Balance. Equal input. He likes it best when two people are working together to make it work. He does not enjoy competing for control, or being beaten down, or ordered around. He will agree to compromise so long as you agree to compromise. A pushover if you treat him right.

X

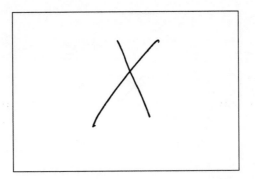

Superlarge

The bigger the X, the more the focus of the relationship will switch to him. Yes, he could overwhelm anybody. He demands that his authority be respected, and seems strangely perturbed when it's not. On the inside, he feels small and is overplaying his hand in order to compensate for perceived inadequacies.

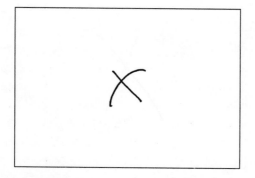

Needs your full attention

He is likely to push himself upon you, demand your time, explanations, and justifications. His needs are extensive, and it's possible that, no matter what you do or how much you say, he will still need more. He looks to others for strength and support but packages his approach in an obvious way.

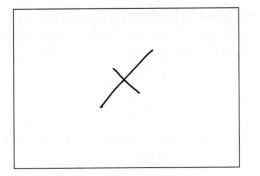

X

Feels shortchanged

He gives too much, that's his problem. He has a basic need to give, give, and keep on giving. He works hard to please—so much so that he is almost guaranteed to feel unappreciated at times. How can you ever match that level of dutiful action? Accept that this is part of his makeup, and do whatever you can in return.

Did his mother do too much for him when he was young?—seems high maintenance; he may appear helpless—but is he really?

 Brings a lot of energy and vibrancy to any relationship, but there will be times when he's not on your wavelength; possibly has one thing and wants another

 Keeps a lot of energy pent up inside; passions and desires are strong yet contained (You may be getting more than you bargained for.)

Y

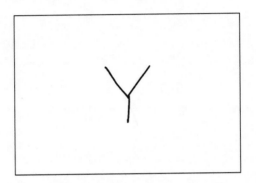

"Where's the party at?"

Oh, joy! This Champagne Charlie knows how to live. He may have a million other flaws, but he sure understands the value of having a good time. He's out to discover new horizons, sights and sounds and tastes. Life won't be dull while he's around. In fact, you may have trouble keeping up with him.

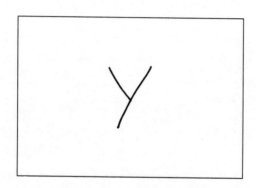

Fun, but responsible

*A hit socially, but look beyond the external signs, dig deeper, and here's someone who takes care of business. Get the work out of the way first, **then** he can have fun. If he ignores this urge, he's going against the grain. You might never know this from meeting him, but he has a dutiful side that needs satisfying too.*

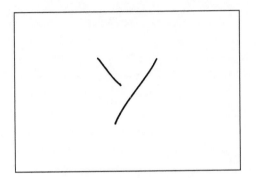

Y

Trying too hard

He's open to a million experiences, and probably wants to sample them all, but in reality he only has time for 999,990. Opportunities slip through his fingers because he can't deal with all the options currently available. In the end, the part of him that has a sense of responsibility wins out. Needs a time-management class.

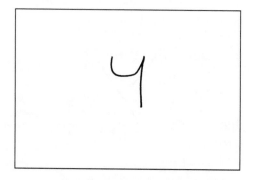

Not ambitious enough

He doesn't believe that he can have everything he dreams of, so he settles for taking the best of what comes his way. He feels lucky if life goes well, but if it doesn't, he may adopt a "Well, of course, nothing ever runs smoothly" attitude to compensate for his low expectations. What's needed is a morale-boosting spring-clean. Out with the negative, in with the positive and expansive.

Little too sensible for his own good; sees no point in getting too excited, since life has dealt him a few rough cards in the past; takes the middle road

 Selective; expectations remain low-key and narrow; too responsible and serious to be the life of the party

 Something gets in the way of a good time; needs to loosen up and offload some mental baggage

 Doesn't fully understand the value of what comes his way; too busy, too involved in getting through the day, lets experience go without appreciating it

Z

Spunky

A dynamic personality that likes to be involved in what's going on. It's important to him that he has his say, puts his point across, and doesn't leave others to make decisions for him. An eager participant rather than an aggressive contender, he may nevertheless come on a little strong at times in his effort to ensure that things go the right way.

Z

Z

Won't miss a trick

In this area at least, the guy's a powerhouse. Critical, involved, always pushing to know, to figure out, to resolve issues, he has a keen eye backed by a keen brain. To outsiders, he may seem irritating, too inquisitive, even a pain in the rear at times. But his motivation is clear—he wants answers and he wants them now—please.

Z

Above the fray

Won't involve himself in unnecessary confrontations. He stands apart, wary, viewing those who come to blows with a certain surprise, as if it's beneath him to join them. In reality, he may be too soft, or too sensible, to participate in arguments or silly roughhousing. He will voice his opinions if he thinks it will help, otherwise he'll stay quiet.

Z

Stalwart

There's restraint here, but also a breaking point. He knows when to hold back and when he's being pushed too far and must retaliate. Unlikely to be the aggressor, he leans more toward reason, although he probably won't shy away from confrontation if it arises. However, he sees little value in being the one to pick a fight.

Grand gestures, fancy displays, likely to strut and put on a performance; when tempers flare, he goes off like a rocket—run for cover!

 Hates battles—he'll sidestep arguments and will inflict damage by gossip or other peaceful means rather than speak face to face

 Considers options and views before fully committing to action; slow to speak out of turn—sees no point in antagonizing others for no good reason

 Too nice for his own good; open to persuasion, a sense of fairness underpins his approach to life—his advance could be slower than others who tear up the rulebook